Debt Determines Your
ENVIRONMENT

Harold Herring

President of The Debt Free Army
& RichThoughts TV

www.HaroldHerring.com

Debt Free Army
Post Office Box 900000, Fort Worth, TX 76161

Debt Determines Your Environment
by Harold Herring

ISBN 978-0-9831779-1-3
Copyright © 2011 by The Debt Free Army
P.O. Box 900000, Fort Worth, Texas 76137
817-222-0011
harold@debtfreearmy.org

Debt Determines Your Environment Table of Contents

Dedication

A Personal Word From
Harold Herring

"Heavenly Father, I want to thank you that you woke me up this morning, clothed me in my right mind, gave me a comfortable place to stay, air to breathe, food to eat, my fine wife Bev, four Godly children, two Godly grand sugars and a Godly daughter-in-love.

"I thank you, Heavenly Father, for giving me the words to write this book. I thank you that I'm anointed to get people out of debt . . . that there's going to be a miracle in my life today and anybody who gets near me . . . or reads this book will have a miracle in their life as well. Amen."

I want to personally thank the author of every book I've ever read that provoked me to think bigger and better thoughts. I am the sum total of all I've read, heard and remembered from these authors and especially, the author of the greatest book ever written . . . our great God Jehovah.

I want to recognize, honor and pay tribute to Brother John Avanzini . . . a close friend, trusted associate, financial mentor and spiritual father. Brother John saw in me what others had not. He is a teacher among teachers . . . and a friend like no other . . . a pastor to pastors. I will always remember that he's the one . . . who God used to bring me to the dance (gave me a chance) . . . and I will always honor him for that.

5

I want to thank our dear friend June Hart, the best Realtor in Tulsa, Oklahoma for the hours she spent reading and giving me her feedback on the rough manuscript. What a precious friend and a mighty woman of God.

I also want to acknowledge the two best parents to draw a breath on planet earth, Harold Herring, Sr. and Annie Ruth Herring. You've always believed in me . . . never given up on me . . . picked me up when I was down and provided the greatest example of Christian living possible.

I want to acknowledge our younger children . . . Abby, Alex and Jamie for the sacrifices they've made in helping me to get the Body of Christ out of debt. You are a joy in my life and I love you with a never ending, never yielding, ever growing love.

I also want to acknowledge my oldest son, Jim, who is the Pastor of Abundant Life Family Church in Watauga, Texas. His understanding of the Word is an inspiration to all who know him.

I also Praise God that I was allowed to wake up this morning next to my fine wife, Bev, the greatest wife ever. She is the epitome of a Proverbs 31 woman who kept faith in me over these many years even when it wasn't easy. She is an anointed teacher of the Word, my co-laborer, a caring pastor, but most of all, she's my best friend. I love you, Honey.

Lastly, I want to acknowledge you . . . because you cared enough about your future to buy this book. I'm ready to take a journey with you to a debt free life.

Foreword

by Dr. Mike Murdock

Few Men Have True Wisdom
...On The Evil of Debt.

Few Men Have True Wisdom . . . On The Evil of Debt.

Harold Herring Has Mastered This Understanding.

That Is Why You Need This Book.

Thousands have broken the chains of Debt because of the Anointing on this Financial Deliverer. His Compassion and His relentless Love for The Family of God . . . has made him a Favorite in World Conferences including The Wisdom Center.

He is Scripturally Sound, Accurate and Integrous. His personal friendship has strengthened, encouraged me and been consistent.

This will become a Handbook you will read daily. It unleashes Hope, exposes the Lies, and stabilizes a workable Strategy for Financial Freedom.

This Book Will Work . . . in your life. We owe great gratitude to our brother for investing his life . . . to Unleash Divine Prosperity Into our lives.

Yours For Financial Victory...
Dr. Mike Murdock

"Did you know when the devil goes to bed at night, before he puts the lights out, he looks under his bed to make sure you aren't there?"

- **Pastor John Hamel**, Evangelist, Hyannis Port, Massachusetts

---

"Having known Brother Harold for many years I can attest to his impeccable character. He is highly respected as a man of God. Through his work with the Debt Free Army, Brother Harold has inspired thousands to come out of financial lack through both Scriptural insight and practical application of the Word."

- **Pastor Duane Broom**, Apoka, Florida

"The first time I saw Harold Herring speak was for another minister. The Holy Spirit revealed to him that a single Mom was present who could not make her house payment. The lady identified herself, Harold and his wife Bev sowed their seed, the need was met and my admiration for the Herrings went into warp drive.

There is no exaggeration in writing that Harold and Bev have helped multiplied thousands reach their goal of a debt-free lifestyle through the principles the Holy Spirit has poured into them. Without question Harold also operates as the Apostle of Encouragement."

- **Pastor Malcolm Burton**, Spring, Texas

"A brilliant man intellectually but he is so casual and at ease in helping us get into wisdom. He's the General in God's Debt Free Army he is a blessing and a gift to me."

- **Dr. Mike Murdock**, The Wisdom Center

Introduction

How To Get The Most Out Of This Book

First, get a pen or pencil and a yellow highlighter.

If this book is to be a blessing to you . . . nearly every page will have notes, asterisk, comments and ideas for practical implementation into your life.

Second, pray.

Ask God to help you understand and activate every scriptural principle taught within the pages of this book . . . so that the fruit of the time you invest . . . will remain and produce a harvest . . . for years to come.

The New Living Translation of John 15:16 says:

"You didn't choose me. I chose you. I appointed you to go and produce lasting fruit, so that the Father will give you whatever you ask for, using my name."

Now I want to show you how to personalize this verse, like I have below.

"Harold didn't choose me. I chose him. I appointed him to go and produce lasting fruit, so that the Father will give Harold whatever he ask[s] for, using my name."

Harold Herring

Third, read the book without distraction.

There may be some books you can read while watching television or with children playing nearby . . . this isn't one of them or it shouldn't be.

Fourth, don't delay in reflecting, recording and recalling the things that you've read and/or heard.

It is a scientific fact that you will forget 50% of what you've read or heard within three hours of reading or hearing it. And sadly, twenty-four hours later you will have forgotten 80% of that information.

If you really want to become debt free, you can. But you must stick to it . . . pursue it and do it.

It's a fact, the scripture says in Mark 4:24 in the Amplified Bible you will receive back more than you sowed.

"And He said to them, Be careful what you are hearing. The measure [of thought and study] you give [to the truth you hear] will be the measure [of virtue and knowledge] that comes back to you--and more [besides] will be given to you who hear."

It's through this process that we can gain insight and deeper revelation into His Word . . . the decisions we need to make and the actions we need to take.

Ready? Let's get started.

Chapter 1

Debt Determines Your
ENVIRONMENT

I was praying during a church service at The Wisdom Center when the Spirit of the Lord stirred these four words in my spirit:

"Debt Determines Your Environment."

I knew that was a profound statement . . . with life-changing implications.

According to dictionary.com the word *environment* is defined as:

"the aggregate [or the total] of surrounding things, conditions, or influences; surroundings"

Does debt influence you by your surroundings? Absolutely!

Debt influences your surroundings if you're living in a house . . . where you're only one step ahead of the foreclosure notices.

Debt influences your surroundings if you're living in a home . . . where you can't afford to get the air conditioner fixed in the heat of summer or you don't have money for heating oil in the cold of winter.

Debt influences your surroundings if you're living in the projects . . . where your kids are in danger of drug users and gunfire.

Debt influences your surroundings if you're living in an apartment building or duplex . . . where you hear every argument and conversation your neighbors have because the walls are so thin.

Debt influences your surroundings if you're living in a place . . . where the cockroaches seem as big as hamsters.

Debt influences your surroundings if your residence is determined by what you can afford as opposed to where you really want to live.

Environment is also defined as "the social and cultural forces that shape the life of a person or a population."

Bombarded by Advertising

Advertising is a powerful social and cultural force. A number of studies point out that the average American is exposed to over 3,000 advertising messages a day . . . this includes radio, TV, internet, billboards or any other medium that promotes a product, cause or lifestyle.

Assuming you sleep eight hours a day, that means during the other sixteen hours a day . . . you are exposed to over 3½ advertising messages every minute of the day. During the year you will be exposed to 1,095,000 advertising messages.

These advertising messages are all geared at selling you a particular product whether you need it or not.

A significant amount of debt is accumulated by people who

are seduced into buying things they cannot afford and then shackled by consumer debt because of peer, social pressure or buying addictions.

If you buy a new car and/or truck because your neighbors have one . . . then you are a casualty of social and advertising seduction.

However, if you can't make the payments on that new vehicle then debt will determine your environment by the car you drive or the one that was repossessed.

If the clothes in your closet are determined by what others, including celebrities, are wearing instead of what you can afford . . . then you have been seduced by society.

If you buy a 64 inch flat panel LED High Def television on the payment plan because your best friend has one . . . or you want everyone to be impressed on Super Bowl Sunday . . . then you have been lured into debt by peer pressure.

Bombarded by Social Pressure

If you're willing to run up your credit card balance so your children can wear name brand clothes and shoes from Saks Fifth Avenue because you never did, then you have been influenced by your environment so you can appear to be changing theirs.

If you put your children in a private and/or Christian school but you can't afford the tuition and fees . . . you may be giving them a greater opportunity but you're digging a bigger financial hole than you'll ever be able to climb out of.

If you buy anything with money you don't have, for the purpose of impressing those in your social circle, then you're a victim of financial and social charades.

13

If you think what you drive . . . where you live . . . what you wear . . . what you have or the stuff you buy but can't pay for . . . validates who you are, then you have allowed debt to determine your environment.

I think it's fair to say that debt is a social and cultural force that has and is continuing to shape the lives of generations. Yes, your choices are shaping your children too.

How It Begins

When my parents were first married they lived in a house that was owned by the farmer for whom they worked as sharecroppers.

The first house they bought was a two-room single-story house of less than 1,000 square feet.

My parents next home was a brick house with two-bedrooms . . . either one of which was bigger than both of the bedrooms in the previous house combined. This home was roughly 1,800 square feet.

The next house my parents purchased, which is their current residence, has three bedrooms, three bathrooms, a big parlor, dining room and a floored attic with another spare bedroom. My parents have lived in this house since 1976 and it has roughly 2,900 square feet.

The housing journey of my parents is similar to that of most Americans of their generation. The average American house size has more than doubled since the 1950's and now stands at nearly 2,500 square feet.

Just after World War II, people began to buy into the notion that owning your own home was the American dream and the best investment you could ever make.

Next came the social progression of owning larger and more expensive houses with fancier and more expensive toys in each house and driveway. This is true whether you now live in a "McMansion" or just a house in the suburbs.

The parental desire for children to have opportunities their parents didn't have has led many to move to better school districts outside the city where the houses are larger and more expensive, the commute more costly and time-consuming, and yes, the appearances needed to keep up with living in such an environment.

Here's the bottom line . . . whatever your reason or motivation . . . debt does determine your environment.

Now is the time to do something about it.

1. Understand why you are where you are.

It's time for a little introspection.

Why did you get yourself into debt? Was it just to buy a house . . . or the right house in the right neighborhood with the right schools?

Are you susceptible to peer pressure when it comes to buying and owning stuff?

Do you buy "things" to relieve the pressure from work, your marriage, or the need to feel that you're making progress in your life?

If you're married, has your journey into the bondage of debt been a solo mission or are both of you responsible?

Do you buy things now, hoping you will have the income in the future to pay for them?

Is your financial plan based on having an available balance on your credit cards?

Are you really counting the cost of the financial decisions you make? Like maintenance and other ongoing costs?

Luke 14:28 in the Message Bible says:

"Is there anyone here who, planning to build a new house, doesn't first sit down and figure the cost so you'll know if you can complete it? If you only get the foundation laid and then run out of money, you're going to look pretty foolish. Everyone passing by will poke fun at you: 'He started something he couldn't finish.'"

You need an honest assessment of why you are where you are.

2. Don't fix the blame . . . solve the problem.

If you're in debt and/or living in financial chaos . . . don't blame anybody else. Man (or woman) up . . . if you mess up . . . take the responsibility for your actions. You can't solve your problem until you realize you have one.

Excuses NEVER solve a problem. Blaming someone else NEVER solves the problem. You're already in a financial hole . . . so stop digging and fussing . . . instead focus on getting out.

John 9:3 in the Message Bible says:

"Jesus said, "You're asking the wrong question. You're looking for someone to blame. There is no such cause-

effect here. Look instead for what God can do. We need to be energetically at work for the One who sent me here, working while the sun shines. When night falls, the workday is over. For as long as I am in the world, there is plenty of light. I am the world's Light."

One more thing . . . SADLY, God sometimes gets the blame . . . when we're the ones who messed up.

Proverbs 19:3 in the Message Bible says:

"People ruin their lives by their own stupidity, so why does God always get blamed?"

The problem with blame is that it's misdirected focus. You're expending mental energy and thought power blaming someone else . . . but you're not using your resources to focus on solving the problem.

So, STOP IT!!

3. Get specific about your current financial situation.

This next point will determine whether or not you're really ready to change your environment.

Taking the time and making the effort to determine the actual state of your financial affairs is a step that often throws folks into a state of procrastination.

The reason many people procrastinate on this step is because they know they're not going to like what they see.

First, if your bills are not already separated into file folders by year . . . do so immediately.

Get a yellow highlighter and mark the existing balance,

interest rate, payoff date and the toll-free number of the creditor. You will need this information in your next step.

Proverbs 27:23 says:

"Be thou diligent to know the state of thy flocks, and look well to thy herds."

It's a sin to make a decision in ignorance when the facts are available. That's the Herring paraphrase of Proverbs 18:13 in The Living Bible which says:

"What a shame — Yes, how stupid to make a decision before knowing the facts."

Second, you've got to know where your money is going. I'm not talking about the big money . . . I'm talking about the small money that you spend every day without even thinking about it.

> "It's a sin to make a decision in ignorance when the facts are available."

Get a small spiral ring notebook (the kind a man can put in his shirt pocket or a woman in her purse). If you're married, both spouses should have one.

For the next thirty days, write down every single penny you spend. Assign each transaction a category. When you add up the total of each category at the end of the thirty day period . . . I'm confident . . . in fact, I guarantee you will find money that you can re-direct into other areas.

4. Create a plan to change your financial environment.

I'm going to give you an absolute fact . . . if you don't have a plan to get out of debt then you will never change your financial environment.

There are a number of plans to help people get out of debt. However, I personally think the Debt Free Army "Master Plan"* is the best one available. I say that based on the success rate of testimonies we've received over the years.

The "Master Plan"* will allow you to create your own personalized out of debt plan. When you've plugged your own numbers into the "Master Plan"* you will know that if you do "this and this and this" . . . by "this" date you will be totally and completely debt free.

However, you must be committed to complete the plan.

In Ecclesiastes 9:10, the first part of that scripture says:

"Whatsoever thy hand finds to do, do it with thy might . . ."

The Bible is telling you that whatever you plan to do, get in there and do it. Be specific about it, and do it.

Proverbs 1:25 in the New International Version says:

"The plans of the diligent lead to profit as surely as haste leads to poverty."

* The **"Master Plan"** is the final and most important step in the **"Debt Terminator Kit"**. For more information on the Debt Terminator and developing your own personalized out-of-debt plan visit the Store at:
www.DebtFreeArmy.org

1 Timothy 4:15 in the New International Version says:

"Give your complete attention to these matters. Throw yourself into your tasks so that everyone will see your progress."

You need to continually monitor your progress and maximize your efforts. Do something toward reaching your goal every day.

> When you don't know what to do next . . . ask God . . . He always knows and has a plan for you.

5. Get God involved in your plan.

If you're in significant debt . . . you may feel a bit overwhelmed . . . even with your personalized Master Plan.

Isaiah 48:17 in the Message Bible says:

"I am God, your God, who teaches you how to live right and well. I show you what to do, where to go."

It's not just enough to ask for His help . . . you need to listen to His voice.

Proverbs 3:5-6 in the Message Bible says:

"Trust God from the bottom of your heart; don't try to figure out everything on your own. Listen for God's voice in everything you do, everywhere you go; he's the one who will keep you on track."

Once you ask for His help . . . listen to His voice . . . then you need to do what He says.

Proverbs 16:3 in the Amplified Bible says:

"Roll your works upon the Lord [commit and trust them wholly to Him; He will cause your thoughts to become agreeable to His will, and] so shall your plans be established and succeed."

The Holy Spirit is here for you. That is why Jesus ascended to the Father and the Holy Spirit stays on earth.

"But the Comforter (Counselor, Helper, Intercessor, Advocate, Strengthener, Standby), the Holy Spirit, Whom the Father will send in My name [in My place, to represent Me and act on My behalf], He will teach you all things. And He will cause you to recall (will remind you of, bring to your remembrance) everything I have told you."
John 14:26

A final thought.

It's time for every born-again child of God to stop debt from determining their environment.

It's time to get started!

Right Now!

It's time for you to get started on your journey to the debt-free lifestyle so you can live in a totally different environment.

Psalm 66:12 in the Amplified Bible says:

"You caused men to ride over our heads [when we were prostrate]; we went through fire and through water, but You brought us out into a broad, moist place [to abundance and

refreshment and the open air].

The King James Version of Psalm 66:12 says that God will bring you into a *"wealthy place."*

Now that's what I call a different kind of environment, the God kind.

Finally, you need to get started . . . right now.

As I was reading back through this book during the final editing I felt led to encourage you to go to our online store and get your own copy of the **Debt Terminator Kit** at:
www.DebtFreeArmy.org/store

Prior Proper Planning Proceeds Success, and the Master Plan and Debt Terminator are excellent tools to help you make the Proper Plan Prior to beginning your journey to a debt free life.

Enter the coupon code:
priorproperplanning

for a 20% discount on the Debt Terminator Kit.

Debt Determines Your Environment

> "Don't put it off; do it now! Don't rest until you do." - Proverbs 6:4 NLT

QUESTIONS:

1.   How does your debt determine your environment?

2.   What's the purpose of all the advertisements that you see each day?

3.   Name the five things you need to do to change your financial environment?

4.   According to Proverbs 6:4, when's the best time for you to begin changing your financial future?

"We [have been] using the *Debt Terminator* series. At that time we had paid off 3 debts and were left with one debt (of over $3000) and our mortgage.

I want to share an update with you. We sowed seed for debt freedom. Our income tax refund was much more than we thought and we were able to pay off the last debt. Now all we owe is our home!

We were also able to put $500 into savings from our refund.

Our next goal is to pay off our mortgage.

Thank you so much for obeying God and taking the Financial Freedom message to everyone."

- L.S., Fort Worth, TX

"We read the book, developed our personal *Master Plan*, signed the commitments to walk debt free and tithe.

Within one week after completing the plan and making our commitments we received $23,000 in an estate settlement that we thought would be $7,000 maximum.

We paid off every debt except the mortgage and that's next."

- T.A., Portland, OR

Chapter 2

Debt Is Evil

"Ye that love the LORD, hate evil: he preserveth the souls of his saints; he delivereth them out of the hand of the wicked."
    Psalm 97:10

In reading Psalm 97:10 . . . the Word of the Lord is very clear.

DEBT IS EVIL

How can I make such a bold statement? Consider the definition of the word *evil* as found in Strong's Concordance (H7451). It means "bad, unpleasant, evil (giving pain, unhappiness, misery)."

Debt is bad.

Debt is unpleasant.

Debt definitely gives pain.

Debt positively brings unhappiness.

Misery is debt's closest friend.

Therefore, as the scripture says . . . if we love God, we should hate debt.

Debt is a subtle mistress . . . it lures you in with the sweet whisper of excitement and pleasure. If you read Proverbs 7 and substitute debt for prostitute, you'll get a clear picture of what I'm referring to.

> Debt is a subtle mistress . . .it lures you in with the sweet whisper of excitement and pleasure.

Debt deceives you into believing that it can be good or bad. That's the justification that one seminar leader used in urging his participants to borrow the equity from their home to invest in day trading.

Wonder how that philosophy works during economic downturns?

Debt is evil . . . 58% of first marriages end in divorce over debt.

Debt is evil . . . when parents (single or otherwise) are working multiple jobs just to make minimum payments.

Debt is evil . . . because some believers are using kingdom money to feed their (interest debt) habit to credit card companies.

Debt is evil . . . when it hinders the preaching of the gospel.

Debt is evil . . . because it creates stress and health problems for those who can't pay their bills.

Debt is evil . . . for the scripture itself says it makes you a slave.

President Abraham Lincoln signed the Emancipation Proclamation on January 1, 1863 but there are still millions of slaves in the US today . . . people bound to "other men" because of debt . . . people who are no longer in control of their own destiny.

Slavery was evil then . . . it's evil now.

Proverbs 22:7 in the Contemporary English Bible says:

"The poor are ruled by the rich, and those who borrow are slaves of moneylenders."

Bottom line . . . if you're in debt . . . **your time is not your own and in my book, that's evil personified**. <u>Should another man dictate how you spend your time without your consent</u>? Your life is all you have on this earth.

If you need more convincing . . . send me an email . . . my purpose is to give you a word of encouragement from your Heavenly Father.

Psalm 97:10 also says *"he delivereth them out of the hand of the wicked."*

No matter how bad your financial circumstances . . . God not only can . . . but **will give you the wisdom necessary to free yourself from the slave merchants of debt and despair**. He will set you free . . . forever.

> The first step is to pray and ask God to forgive you for any past financial foolishness.

QUESTIONS:

1. What does Psalm 97:10 say about debt?

2. How is the word *evil* defined according to Strong's Concordance?

3. Who is Debt's closest friend?

4. What is the first step you have to take to experience freedom from the slave merchants of debt and despair?

Chapter 3

Are You Under The Influence?

Make no mistake about it . . . Debt is slavery.

Galatians 5:1 says:

"Christ has set us free to live a free life. So take your stand! Never again let anyone put a harness of slavery on you."

Need more proof? Consider the words of Proverbs 22:7 in the Contemporary English Version of the Bible:

"The poor are ruled by the rich, and those who borrow are slaves of moneylenders."

If the money you earn each week is not your own . . . free from the demands of creditors . . . then you're a slave to the moneylenders.

Dictionary.com defines *slave* as:

"a person entirely under the domination of some influence or person."

If every penny you make is designated for making monthly or minimum payments then you . . . are under the influence of someone else.

Now that's an interesting thought: "under the influence." Some people get "under the influence" with liquor, beer, wine, or illegal or prescription drugs.

There are millions of Christians who would never even be tempted to be "under the influence" of drugs or alcoholic beverages but they're definitely "under the influence" of Visa, Master Card, Discover, American Express, and dozens of other retailers, shopping networks and websites.

> When you're in debt . . . you're "under the influence" of creditors.

When you're in debt . . . you're "under the influence" of creditors. Oftentimes your servitude to the lenders will determine your response to the things God wants you to do, the places He wants you to sow, and where He wants you to go.

When you're "under the influence" your thought processes, your speech, your reaction time, your body responses are all controlled by something other than God.

When you're "under the influence" you can make unwise choices that may seem exhilarating at the moment but when you sober up, you can't believe that you made such a fool out of yourself.

There are people who make unwise choices in the debts they incur. At the moment, it seemed exhilarating to own the big High-Definition Flat Screen LED TV so you can watch the beads of sweat on the brow of your favorite National Football League player . . . BUT there is going to come a moment when you realize that you bit off more than you can chew (afford).

You're "under the influence" . . . when you have to work two jobs just to make ends meet no matter how much you enjoy watching a football game.

You're "under the influence" . . . when both you and your spouse have to sacrifice time with your family to make payments on the new truck and car payments.

You're "under the influence" . . . when you can't afford to put your children in Christian school because your extra money is tied up in interest payments.

You're "under the influence" . . . when you even consider withholding the tithe from God to make payments that are past due.

You're "under the influence" . . . when you aren't free to give what God tells you to give when and where He tells you to give it.

Being "under the influence" of debt can be just as addictive as alcohol or drugs.

I have written a lot of blogs found on *www.debtfreearmy.org* about people who are compulsive shoppers and spenders. If you finance or charge something you don't really need when you are already making payments with finance charges attached . . . with money you don't have yet . . . then you're definitely "under the influence."

Alcoholics and druggies will beg, borrow, and even demean themselves for the money necessary to buy a drink or get a fix. In short, they will do whatever it takes to feed their habit. The same is true with compulsive spenders and shoppers.

Sadly, there are millions of **Christians** who think

themselves okay because they are not "under the influence" of alcohol or drugs but fall prey to being "under the influence" to a string of credit cards.

I could go on . . . but I'm sure you understand what I mean by being "under the influence" of creditors. Now let's go a little further.

We've established that those who are in debt . . . are called "slaves" in the Bible . . . they are "under the influence" of the moneylenders.

Let's look at Galatians 5:1 again.

"Christ has set us free to live a free life. So take your stand! Never again let anyone put a harness of slavery on you."

As I read and re-read this verse in five different translations, I was stirred by how many believers I've talked to over the years got out of debt using our Debt Free Army materials only to get back into debt again. Frankly speaking, that tells me they're still "under the influence."

> It's just not enough to get out of debt . . .
> **you must STAY OUT OF DEBT.**

First, purpose in your heart that you will NEVER under any circumstances yield to the allure of debt again. It will take discipline to keep you from operating your finances under the influence of the creditors but if anyone has the power available to do it . . . it would be a Christian under the control of the Holy Spirit.

Second, once you get out of debt and out from under the influence of the creditors . . . cancel all your credit

cards except one. It's beneficial to have one card to use for rental cars and hotel deposits while traveling. However, you might ask your credit card company to reduce your credit limit to a reasonable amount based on your personal situation.

Put your credit card cancellation request in writing. It will give you a permanent record plus it will lessen your temptation when the new credit card applications arrive. Safeguard yourself from the temptation of getting "under the influence" again.

Matthew 26:41 in the New Living Translation says:

"Keep watch and pray, so that you will not give in to temptation. For the spirit is willing, but the body is weak!"

Shred all new credit card offers that come into your mailbox or computer inbox.

Simply said, if you don't have a credit card . . . you greatly reduce the temptation to get back "under the influence" of the moneylenders.

Third, create a plan for when you get out of debt.

Ask yourself. . .

What's the one thing you would do if you were debt free?

Where should you sow your seed once it's been liberated from the moneylenders?

Who would you bless if you weren't under the influence of debt?

Where should you invest? Will He direct you to stocks, bonds, mutual funds, or real estate?

I strongly encourage you to create a plan so you can follow the plan of your new goal when you become debt free. It will create extra enthusiasm for seeing your debt freedom plan to completion.

I have found that people who don't have a plan are more easily moved back into debt because they're seeking what's familiar to them. They yield to their past comforts and move back "under the influence."

My prayer is that you will never go down that road again.

The only way to stay free of the influence of the moneylenders is to TAKE A STAND and vow that with God's help you will never again wear the harness of slavery to debt.

I was just reminded of Psalm 94:16 which is an appropriate parting thought.

"Who will rise up for me against the wicked? Who will take a stand for me against evildoers?"

Ask yourself. . .

What's the one thing you would do if you were debt free?

QUESTIONS:

1. Are you "under the influence" of someone else? A creditor?

    _____

    _____

    _____

    _____

2. Being "under the influence" of debt can be almost as addictive as _____ and _____.

3. What are three ways outlined in this chapter to keep you out of debt?

    _____

    _____

    _____

4. A future investment and sowing plan will help you visualize your goals as well as energize your

    _____

5. What is the only way to stay free of the influence of the money lenders?

    _____

    _____

    _____

    _____

". . . We have paid off 8-10 department store credit cards, sent them all back and canceled our accounts. We have also closed our bank credit card and home equity accounts.

Also, two other medium sized bills have been paid off.

Next year we plan . . . to give to God the way we've always wanted to. We're so thankful to the Debt Free Army."

- F.J.G., Phoenix, AZ

"This ministry taught my family about finances and helped us to get out of debt and we're continuing to do so."

-A.S., Fort Dix, NJ

Chapter 4

They're Plotting
Evil Against You

We have established a scriptural foundation to prove that debt is evil . . . now you need to understand there are people who are plotting against you and your economic well-being. They may not be personally aware but they are working for the dark side.

Proverbs 14:22 in the New International Version says:

"Do not those who plot evil go astray? But those who plan what is good find love and faithfulness."

This scripture got me thinking about creditors . . . companies who spend big money to figure out how to get you in debt and keep you there.

They don't think about you as an individual. To them you are a statistic. A certain amount of people are going to "fall for these tactics." As P.T. Barnum said, "A sucker is born every minute." They merely want you to be "their sucker."

I was reminded that the purveyors of credit so often target people who are just barely making ends meet. They **zero in on the person who can only make the minimum payments without any real hope (in the natural) of ever paying off their debts**.

It's pretty obvious they are targeting these folks because they will make more money on them over time. These are the folks who think in terms of "can I afford this monthly payment?" without thought of the overall price of the item they're buying.

It's a sad situation but nonetheless true. **Which customer do you think the credit card company prefers?**

Would they select the single mother who is working two jobs just to continue making the minimum monthly payments or the person who pays off their credit card balance in full each month?

> It's obvious . . . **credit card companies make more money on the people who can only make the minimum payments each month.**

The credit card companies <u>carefully study the profiles of certain socio-economic groups to target those people who will end up paying them more in interest</u>.

The customer profile includes people who can barely keep their head above the financially troubled waters . . . these are the customers they target first.

There are many companies who just want a fair and honest profit . . . but what about those who profile and <u>then target certain groups to secure customers who have a credit addiction</u>? Those are the ones I'm addressing because they need a good case of salvation.

So when I read *"Do not those who plot evil go astray. . .?"* I thought of credit card companies and the credit card divisions of many of the major banks.

They plot evil . . . they plot debt . . . they plot to ensnare unsuspecting consumers into a lifestyle of misery and despair. That's evil . . . pure and simple.

The number one corporate owner of the Payday Loan Centers, which charge exorbitant rates to low income customers, is a bank.

A typical payday loan for $100 with a $15 fee carries an interest rate of 391% APR. That's right 391% interest.

In my opinion . . . it's evil and just plain wrong to take advantage of people who can least afford it.

Over the past few years, many of the major banks and financial institutions have begun reaping what they've sown.

There is a law of sowing and reaping, and it applies to everything . . . money included.

If you plot to take advantage of people . . . **profiling people with the full knowledge of the economic consequences they will face** . . . that's sowing seeds that are just evil . . . and the banks who have made millions/billions off these type practices are now reaping a harvest of the evil they've sown.

Am I being too hard on them? Not a chance.

If debt is evil and the scripture proves that it is, **then those who plan evil deserve what they gct.**

Do not fall into collusion with those planning evil . . . rather devote your life to fulfilling the last part of Proverbs 14:22 NIV:

". . . But those who plan what is good find love and faithfulness."

Plan what is good . . . don't get yourself into debt . . . but rather be used by God to be a blessing to others.

When you're debt free . . . you've got choices . . . you become wise and stay clear of a credit card company's profile . . . you are free to sow seed that will guarantee you a harvest (Galatians 6:7). You're free to enjoy life as God planned it for His children.

> Get out of debt so you don't fall victim as "...a slave to the moneylenders."
>
> - Proverbs 22:7 CEV

Free yourself from those who plot how to keep you addicted to credit. You are not destined to live a life of financial bondage.

Kick the debt habit . . . kick the evilness of debt out of your life and use God's power to resist those who plot evil (debt) against you. **You can do it!**

QUESTIONS:

1. According to Psalm 97:10, those that love the Lord will be delivered out of the hands of the wicked and their souls preserved if they do what?

   _____

   _____

   _____

2. What is a close friend of debt?

   _____

   _____

   _____

3. What will those who plan good find?

   _____

   _____

   _____

4. Who do the credit card companies target so those people will end up paying more interest?

   _____

   _____

   _____

5. Removing yourself from underneath debt will keep you from becoming a slave to whom?

   _____

   _____

   _____

"We drove about 4 ½ hours to get to your conference, but it was well worth the drive. We so much appreciated the messages delivered and the spirit with which they were delivered

. . . we have managed to pay off one small bill and have almost paid off another retail store bill since the conference (10 days earlier).

. . . we purchased the Debt Terminator . . . we have been working through "The Master Plan"*. Interestingly, we located some expenditures that were blind spots to us and now . . . we are dealing with them appropriately

. . . a plan is in place to do Debt Elimination including helping someone else pay off their debts."

- J.B., Kingman, AZ

* "The Master Plan" is the final and most important step in the "Debt Terminator Kit." A program designed to get you out of debt rapidly and keep you out of debt. For more information visit The Store at:
www.debtfreearmy.org

Chapter 5

A Fool And His Money Are Soon Parted

A fool and his money are soon parted.

The first time I heard that expression was when I was about 10 years old working at my father's Western Auto store in eastern North Carolina.

It was summertime and a friend of mine had been working in tobacco. In case you don't know it . . . that's hot, nasty work but it pays good money. You have to wear long sleeve shirts in the summertime heat because there is a sticky gum on the tobacco leaves that adheres to every surface it touches.

Imagine ripping a dozen band-aids off the hairiest part of your arm . . . that's what it feels like when you "try" to get tobacco gum off your body. It's stays permanently on clothes.

Back to the story . . . this young friend of mine had been working in tobacco and the money was burning a hole in his pocket. He came into the store and started filling his arms with every bicycle accessory imaginable.

When he walked to the counter, he laid down a horn, headlight, mud flaps, streamers and a few other things. When my father rang it up on the cash register he told Bobby that the total was $9.97.

Bobby patted his tobacco gum covered shirt pockets, then the front and back pockets of his blue jeans. Unable to find his money, he repeated the process and this time found the money tucked in the bottom corner of his right back pocket. His money was rolled and folded into the size of a postage stamp.

> "The wise man saves for the future, but the foolish man spends whatever he gets."
>
> - Proverbs 21:20 TLB

Bobby carefully unfolded the tobacco gum covered ten dollar bill for my father who handed three pennies back to Bobby. I'll never forget how Bobby looked down at his three pennies lying on the counter.

He then looked up at my father and said, "A fool and his money are soon parted."

I've heard the same sentiments expressed by a number of people who've attended my seminars over the years. They bought stuff on an impulse only to be left with the consequences of a staggering debt.

Proverbs 21:20 in The Living Bible says:

"The wise man saves for the future, but the foolish man spends whatever he gets."

People spend money in some rather foolish ways . . . and just for the record . . . financial foolishness is no respecter of persons. People are foolish regardless of age, gender, race, ethnicity, or education earned.

Credit addiction is not limited to those who make little

money. I come across people who make $25,000 a year and owe $100,000 and those who make $100,000 a year and owe half a million dollars.

Financial insanity just manifests in different ways, depending on an individual's choices, and sadly, it sometimes depends on socio-economic conditions. Poor people will often spend money on things they hope will help them escape their situation, i.e. lottery tickets and risky schemes.

<u>None of the millionaires that I personally know ever buy lottery tickets</u>. They are looking for investments with a high ROI "return on investment." They realize the odds of winning a lottery are so astronomical they'd rather invest their money in something with more of a guaranteed return.

However, there are still millionaires who buy multiple houses and cars overextending themselves with foolish purchases. Everyone makes mistakes. It's how fast we wise up and correct our mistakes that's important.

Understand that having a bunch of letters or numbers after your last name doesn't make you wise and successful. Money can buy you an education but not wisdom.

Proverbs 17:16 in the New Living Translation says:

"Of what use is money in the hand of a [self-confident] fool to buy skillful and godly wisdom--when he has no understanding or heart for it?"

The language in the Message Bible is even more explicit.

"What's this? Fools out shopping for wisdom! They wouldn't recognize it if they saw it!"

I have seen studies that show the more education a person has the more likely they are to spend themselves into trouble . . . believing they have the ability to "think" themselves out of their financial mess.

There is an old expression that "some people are just educated beyond their intelligence."

Please understand I'm not picking on any one group of people . . . I'm just saying that having an education doesn't make you wise . . . only the Word of God does.

> "Some people are just educated beyond their intelligence."

Of all the things taught in schools, there is little on practical money issues. Unfortunately, that is also true in churches. Of all the topics in the Bible, **there are more scriptures dealing with money issues than faith, healing or salvation combined**. God must have known we'd need financial wisdom.

That's why a fool is defined as someone who lives apart from God and His wisdom. It's just that simple.

Proverbs 1:7-9 in The Living Bible says:

"How does a man become wise? The first step is to trust and reverence the Lord!

Only fools refuse to be taught. Listen to your father and mother. What you learn from them will stand you in good stead; it will gain you many honors."

If you're tired of living in debt and lack, there comes a point where you have to say enough is enough and begin to take control of your own financial destiny following the wisdom of the Word.

Proverbs 9:6 in The Living Bible says it this way:

"Leave behind your foolishness and begin to live; learn how to be wise."

Proverbs 12:15 in The Living Bible says:

"... a wise man will listen to others."

It's been said that the biggest fool in town is the person who fools himself.

When you are in an economic mess . . . it's time for you regardless of your social or economic status to face the financial facts . . . and move toward the financial wisdom found in God's Word.

Proverbs 14:8 in The Living Bible says:

"The wise man looks ahead. The fool attempts to fool himself and won't face facts."

If you've read this far, then I know you've made a commitment to wisdom . . . that is leaving financial foolishness behind . . . and moving into God's plan for your economic well-being.

Now that's something to shout about.

QUESTIONS:

1. According to the Word of God the wise man
    _____ for the future.

2. Why do people spend money on the lottery and/or risky schemes?

    _____
    _____
    _____
    _____

3. What does ROI mean?

    _____ _____ _____

4. What does the Bible teach more about than faith, healing and salvation combined?

    _____

5. When will you begin to take control of your financial destiny?

    _____
    _____

Chapter 6

You Can't Have It Both Ways

"No man can serve two masters: for either he will hate the one, and love the other; or else he will hold to the one, and despise the other. Ye cannot serve God and mammon."
Matthew 6:24

Mammon . . . a word which only appears in four verses of the King James version of the Bible yet it's often misunderstood and misquoted by well-meaning folks.

For most of my life, I heard the biblical misinterpretation because *mammon* was used as an excuse for being poor and broke. The common thought was:

"Money is evil because you can't serve God and mammon."

Well meaning but misled pastors would say, "God warned us about money because He said you can't serve Him and *mammon*."

I've discovered that the folks who incorrectly interpret this verse . . . don't really understand what the word means.

So let's begin with the basics.

In Strong's Concordance the word *mammon* (G3126) is the

Greek word *mamōnas* and it means "**riches (where it is personified and is opposed to God).**"

This verse is actually saying that money is mammon when it's a rival to God . . . when it opposes His desires and plans for His children.

What kinds of riches are opposed to God? Simply said, any riches that are used to prevent the children of God from fulfilling His plan and divine destiny for giving them a rich and satisfying life.

Here's a bit of enlightening history for you.

Would it be fair to say that the interest you're paying on your debt . . . would be riches that are opposed to God . . . because it's preventing you from walking in financial freedom?

It is said the Syrians served a god called Mammon.

Additionally, the Syrians were the first people to create a system of loaning money.

When you're up to your eyeballs in debt . . . paying interest . . . continually worried because your money runs out before the month does . . . then your "riches" are being used in a way that is opposed to God's purposes.

The Mammon god says . . . **you can afford the monthly payment plan** . . . but isn't that opposed to God's purpose?

The Mammon god says . . . **you can buy now, pay later** . . . but isn't that's opposed to God's purpose?

The Mammon god says . . . **you deserve to buy yourself**

something special . . . **you've worked hard** . . . you deserve a break today (not referring to McDonalds).

The Mammon god is selfish . . . our God is generous.

The Mammon god says if you have the right credit cards, cars, home, and job, you will be accepted by the right

> If you're buying things with money you don't have, then you are trusting the world's system instead of the Word system.

people . . . **but mammon lies** . . . **deceives** . . . **entraps** . . . **and destroys**.

If you're paying interest on those things you've bought, then you're putting your trust, confidence, and faith in the credit card company or lender and not waiting or believing God will provide.

Are you serving God . . . or are you serving the lenders . . . paying them interest . . . following their plans for your life?

Who are you serving? Are you serving God or debt, the *Mammon* **god of this world?**

And the real question is . . . does the system of mammon steal your freedom to do the things God has called you to do?

The mammon system lures you into debt. Make no mistake about it . . . **debt is spending money you haven't earned**.

It's when you're working to satisfy MasterCard's minimum payments and your money is not your own, neither is it available to God's Kingdom . . . but rather, it's serving mammon.

Make no mistake about it . . . when you're in debt to the mammon system, you have indeed become **a slave to an institution that hopes you never quit paying for their rich lavish lifestyle**.

2 Timothy 2:4 in the Amplified Bible says:

"No soldier when in service gets entangled in the enterprises of [civilian] life; his aim is to satisfy and please the one who enlisted him."

Here's the question you need to ask yourself, How free are you to serve God and establish His covenant in the earth?

I want to ask you that question again. How free are you to serve God?

When you're working two jobs just to keep the collection agency from your door, you're not available to God.

> How free are you to serve God and establish His covenant in the earth?

The New Living Translation of 2 Timothy 2:4 says:

"Soldiers don't get tied up in the affairs of civilian life, for then they cannot please the officer who enlisted them."

The King James Version says:

"No man that warreth entangleth himself with the affairs of this life; that he may please him who hath chosen him to be a soldier."

The Hebrew word for *borrow* means **"entangle or intertwine."**

When we entangle ourselves with creditors or the mammon system to the point that we've lost our freedom to do what God has called us to do, then we're not free.

We have so much **stuff** we need to **take care of**, pay for, **insure**, organize, **fix**, worry about, and **keep track of**, we've lost sight of what God saved us for. It wasn't just so we could go to heaven when we die.

If your pastor asks you to go on a mission's trip but you tell him you can't afford to miss a week of work . . . then you're not really free.

If one of your children wants you to be the chaperone on a school field-trip but you can't because you need the income from your second job to help make the car payment . . . then you're not free.

If you're sitting in a church service, a Debt Free Army seminar, or another ministry meeting and God stirs you to give an offering of $1,000 . . . but you can't because of the mortgage payment, the home equity loan, the credit card bills . . . then you're not free. You're into the mammon system.

Frederick Saunders, a recipient of the Victoria Cross which is the highest and most prestigious award for gallantry in the face of the enemy that can be awarded to a citizen of the British Commonwealth, once said:

"Mammon is the largest slave-holder in the world."

Proverbs 22:7 in the Contemporary English Version of the Bible says:

"The poor are ruled by the rich, and those who borrow are slaves of the moneylenders."

Moneylenders and the system of mammon are one and the same.

Here's the bottom line . . . if you're up to your eyeballs in debt . . . then you're not free to give when God says "Give" or go when God says "Go". . . you're a servant of the mammon system.

When you're **not** free to do what God says when He says it . . .

you're serving the wrong master.

When you're not free to do what God says when He says it . . . you're serving the wrong master . . . that's unscriptural and contrary to the plan of God.

The enemy knows this and that's why he lures unsuspecting believers into the bondage of debt. **He wants you serving the lender . . . paying high interest rates . . . supporting the mammon system that's opposed to the plans and purposes of our Heavenly Father.**

Riches are neither good nor bad . . . it's what you do with them that determines their character. **The riches passing through your hands reflects who you are.**

The American writer, Logan Pearsall Smith, said:

"Those who set out to serve both God and mammon soon discover that there is no God."

You have a choice to make . . . do you want to be free? **You can't serve God and mammon . . . you can't have it both ways.**

The Bible says when you Serve God . . . Obey God . . . then you will live long and prosper (Proverbs 3).

Debt Determines Your Environment

QUESTIONS:

1.   Does man have the ability to serve two masters?

      _____

2.   In your own life, have you ever tried to give two things your complete attention and found that one always wins over the other? What did you regard more highly?

      _____

      _____

      _____

3.   What is the Strong's Concordance definition of the of the word *mammon*?

      _____

      _____

      _____

4.   What kinds of riches are opposed to God?

      _____

      _____

      _____

5.   Who were the first group of people to create a system of loaning money? _____

6.   The Mammon god is _____ but our God is _____.

"I sat with Harold at the Philadelphia Debt Free Army Rally. When I left my home Saturday morning I had twenty dollars in my pocket to place in your offering. What I hadn't counted on was hearing God speak to me . . .

To make a long story short, God . . . said to give [an] amount which I could not afford. I prayed about it . . . you got my pledge and I got a life-changing experience. It seemed like a fair trade to me . . . [But] I [had to] scrape up the money to fulfill my pledge . . . and [hope] my wife [wouldn't] kill me for making the pledge.

When I arrived home I found a check for $5,600 which arrived quite unexpectedly. Pledge problem solved, wife problem, bill problem (at least one) solved. Amen.

I want you to consider me a follower of everything you do. This has changed my outlook and my life forever and I thank God for sending you. I love the vision you have for your ministry and its projects and your passion for what you do."

- J.H., Alburtis, PA

Chapter 7

Are You A Booty Call?

Okay, don't judge me until you finish reading this chapter because the word *booty* is used in the Bible anywhere between 3 and 8 times depending on which translation you use.

The word *booty* according to Strong's Concordance means to "plunder" or "take spoils."

Growing up I was fascinated by the tales of pirates and the swashbucklers who sought their booty (treasure) by whatever means possible.

I think it's fair to say . . . that <u>taking the *booty* means taking something that doesn't belong to you</u> . . . or that which may be given up under false promises or pretenses.

Habakkuk 2:7 in the Amplified Bible says:

"Shall [your debtors] not rise up suddenly who shall bite you, exacting usury of you, and those awake who will vex you [toss you to and fro and make you tremble violently]? <u>Then you will be booty for them</u>."

In the contemporary vernacular . . . a *booty call* is when someone initiates a solicitation (phone call) to have an illicit, unscriptural, sometimes sexual relationship with someone else.

Generally the person making the call only has their personal pleasure or gain in mind with no regard for how the visit will impact the person being called. The caller will befriend the person being called as long as it benefits them. There is certainly no long commitment in their mind, much less a desire to be around when times are tough.

A *booty call* gone bad can result in an unwanted pregnancy and the responsibility of caring for a child for 18-22 years, if not longer.

Now let's look at *booty calls* from a different perspective.

Have you ever had 'friends' who were close to you when times were good . . . only to find them nowhere to be found when the road you were traveling got bumpy?

> Fair-weather friends are gone faster than a gallon of Rocky Road ice cream at a church picnic in July.

These are the kind of friends who want to join you when you are enjoying life and all it has to offer, as long as things are going the way they want. These friends are excited when you dine at the finest restaurants, stay at the swankiest hotels, or buy that new video game system, Louis Vitton purse, new set of golf clubs or Versace dress and Armani suit. These friends are even happy when you go buy your groceries as long as they can come along and look good riding in your Mercedes.

But what happens to these friends when you can't or choose not to do the things you've always done?

Sadly, you learn that these fair-weather friends are gone

faster than a gallon of Rocky Road ice cream at a church picnic in July.

Who are these friends?

They are the manufacturers / advertisers / credit card companies who are making *booty calls* on unsuspecting believers 24/7.

Have you ever noticed how they tell you how priceless life is . . . until you've maxed out your credit card? Then the funny commercials, cute sayings, and alluring ads move on to make their next *booty call* because they are no longer interested in you.

The unsuspecting believer . . . the one who's been seduced into debt . . . finds himself/herself with an unwanted birth . . . a bundle of debt that's going to hang around for 18-22 years or longer.

These 'friends' who sent you credit cards applications, encouraged you to open your charge accounts, and revolving credit were close to you when times were good. They would call you . . . lure you into the latest and greatest deal . . . but when the road got bumpy . . . and you couldn't feed their habit . . . they were gone quicker than my Momma's banana pudding at a family reunion.

The New Living Translation states Habakkuk 2:7 rather plainly.

*"Suddenly, **your debtors will take action. They will turn on you and take all you have**, while you stand trembling and helpless."*

When you can't satisfy your 'friends' . . . not only will they abandon you . . . they will take action against you . . . without the slightest bit of remorse.

You may have been treated like their very best friend, but now you're just a faint memory of a *booty call* that's come and gone.

Make no mistake about it . . . these booty callers do not care if you can't make your minimum monthly payment . . . they don't care if you lose your job . . . they don't care if your spouse left you and the kids with no means of support . . . they don't care if your sales are off . . . they will leave you faster than you can sing "you've lost that loving feeling" when they can't use you anymore.

> *"Suddenly, your debtors will take action. They will turn on you and take all you have, while you stand trembling and helpless."*
>
> Habakkuk 2:7

The next time a credit card company gives you a *booty call* . . . to plunder your hard earned-money . . . **you know what to do**.

Sing a little Ray Charles to them ". . . *Hit the road Jack and don't come back . . . no more!*"

QUESTIONS:

1.   How does Habakkuk 2:7 define booty?

_____

_____

_____

2.   What happens to fair-weather friends when you decide not to indulge in the things you once did, such as fine restaurants, nice suits, and exciting gifts?

_____

_____

_____

3.   Have you ever had a fair-weather friend? How did the relationship impact you? Was it difficult to extricate yourself from the situation? What did you learn from the experience?

_____

_____

_____

_____

4.   What should you do next time a credit card company gives you a booty call?

_____

_____

_____

_____

"I attended a Debt Free Rally...I sowed a small seed of less than $2.00. It was all I had at the time.

Brother Harold taught on the principles of being debt free and I received it. I am happy to report that I was able to pay off a loan from a predatory lender company.

I thank you for the tools and information that took me to a new level in my kingdom thinking."

- K.P, Mobile, AL

"Thanks to your ministry . . . I am debt free and own my home and 2 trailers . . . Your ministry was my only light in a very dark time in my life."

- F.B., Tipton, IN

Chapter 8

Buy Now and Pay Later
and Later and Later

Watch out for the hook . . . the trick . . . the trap. It looks good . . . pleasing to the eye and yes, it will tingle your senses . . . but it will also put you in bondage quicker than you can say, "Where Do I Sign?"

"No Interest Until January
(A Year 2 or 3 Years From Now)."

Those <u>words have snared many an unsuspecting believer into financing their future</u>.

Okay, the year may change but the bondage doesn't. **The real danger of this type of financing or any kind of debt is that it presumes your finances will be better tomorrow than they are today**. That's dangerous thinking. It presumes you will not hit any bumps in the road between now and when the next payment or final payment comes due.

Advertising executives understand and exploit the mentality that thrives on:

"90 Days Same As Cash."
"No Payments Until July 1st Next Year"

For the cash-strapped, it "feels" like a reprieve from

63

bondage. It's meant to "look" like a way to not be in prison to your finances any more . . . but it is no "get out of jail" card. It just ends up being another cement block tied around your ankles.

I can assure you that salesmen . . . especially selling big ticket items . . . have been schooled in how to make things appealing . . . to draw you in . . . to close the sale.

The salesperson's basic motivation is to get "their" money out of "your" pocket. That phrase is actually used in sales training classes and sales motivated books. I want what I just said to sink in. **At the moment, it's your money in your pocket but their job is to get that money out of your pocket and into theirs.**

Am I cynical? No, not at all. I'm being very factual and I understand sales.

I used to teach sales and sales training. I've read dozens of books and listened to hundreds of CDs on the subject. At one time, I had over 1,000 people in my insurance sales organization.

I understand the motivation . . . the strategies . . . how to close the sale by answering all your objections . . . to get the person thinking and dreaming about possibilities of owning and wanting the product.

Fortunately, I sold something a person needs to buy . . . like proper life insurance but the same tactics are used to sell a lot of unsuspecting people things they certainly don't need.

It's a lot easier to talk someone into buying something they'd really "like to own" but know they shouldn't be buying because they can't possibly afford it."

The mission for the sales person at the car dealership or electronics store is to talk you into finding a way you can swing this fabulous deal. They are there to help you rationalize how you can somehow make it work.

Then you'll own this unbelievable 'thing' that you never thought you could afford . . . because you couldn't!

Remember Habakkuk 2:7 in the Amplified Bible:

"Shall [your debtors] not rise up suddenly who shall bite you, exacting usury of you, and those awake who will vex you [toss you to and fro and make you tremble violently]? Then you will be booty for them."

It's kind of like going fishing. The fish may be leery of humans but they become distracted by the fishing lure that darts in and out of the water . . . yet nothing distracts the fisherman from pulling that fish in the boat. Don't be caught like a fish.

> The real danger of any kind of debt is that it presumes your finances will be better tomorrow than they are today.
>
> Never ever make a spending decision based on presumed future income.

If you ever begin to think . . . "I'm suppose to get a raise in six months" or "We could pay this off with our income tax refund" . . . don't! **Never ever make a spending decision based on presumed future income**.

That is a costly and even unscriptural assumption.

In fact, let me say it one more time . . . **Never ever make any spending decision based on presumed future income**.

James 4:13-15 in the Amplified Bible says:

"Come now, you who say, <u>Today or tomorrow</u> we will go into such and such a city and spend a year there and carry on our business and make money.

*Yet **you do not know [the least thing] about what may happen tomorrow**. What is the nature of your life? You are [really] but a wisp of vapor (a puff of smoke, a mist) that is visible for a little while and then disappears [into thin air].*

*You ought instead to say, **If the Lord is willing, we shall live and we shall do this or that [thing]**."*

If there is one thing we can know for sure . . . nothing is certain in the current economic climate . . . that is why we must base our future on the Word of God and His economy.

That's why you should heed the words of Proverbs 27:1 in Message Bible:

"Don't brashly announce what you're going to do tomorrow; you don't know the first thing about tomorrow."

There is no way you can be assured of anything in the world's economy . . . if you disagree, ask the folks who've lost their homes or millions of dollars in the stock market or their entire retirement due to swindles by highly regarded financial gurus.

It's important for every believer to understand about these NO INTEREST FOR YEARS programs . . . the companies offering the deal are playing the numbers. For them . . . it's certainly not a gamble.

It is a statistical fact that over 70% of the people who sign up for these No Interest Deferred Payment plans either miss or are late on a payment. Read the fine print yourself. On many of these offers, if you miss just one payment over the period of the contract or are late just one time, your interest rate will skyrocket to over 25% (in some states as high as 37%) . . . and ALL the interest will be added back into the amount of the loan.

> Just remember, it's easy to get into these
>
> BUY NOW PAY LATER
>
> plans but it's tough getting out.

The merchant who is offering you this 'seemingly too-good-to-be-true deal' is going to sell your contract to a finance company and, like Dracula, they will be draining your life-blood in no time. These contracts are not to be entered into lightly.

The scripture confirms that it's a sin to make a decision in ignorance . . . that's the Herring paraphrase of Proverbs 18:13 which actually says:

"He that answereth a matter before he heareth it, it is folly and shame unto him."

The Contemporary English Version of Proverbs 18:13 says:

"It's stupid and embarrassing to give an answer before you listen."

Just get the facts:

Before you sign on the dotted line . . . or even get close to it . . . ask the Holy Spirit's guidance if this purchase is right for you . . . if you can afford it . . . ask if it is contrary to God's plan for your life.

Consider the following scriptures.

Proverbs 1:5 says:

"A wise man will hear, and will increase learning; and a man of understanding shall attain unto wise counsels."

Proverbs 1:7 says:

"The fear of the Lord is the beginning of knowledge: but fools despise wisdom and instruction."

Proverbs 20:27 in the New Living Translation says:

"The Lord's searchlight penetrates the human spirit, exposing every hidden motive."

Just remember, it's easy to get into these BUY NOW PAY LATER plans but it's tough getting out.

QUESTIONS:

1. What four words have snared many unsuspecting believers into *financing* their future?

    _____ _____ _____ _____

2. The salesperson's basic motivation is to do what?

    _____
    _____
    _____
    _____

3. Never ever make a spending decision based on _____ income.

4. What percentage of people opt for a No Interest Deferred Payment plan but find themselves paying late or missing a payment?

    _____

5. Is there a big purchase you need to make in the near future? Have you asked the Lord if the purchase is right for you? Are you heeding His words? *(see Appendix for more information)*

    _____
    _____
    _____
    _____

In 1997, the first Debt Free Army Rally was held in Memphis, Tennessee. From that meeting, Emma became a member of the Debt Free Army. With only a high school education and a disabled husband, she took the materials and came completely out of debt and began putting money into a retirement plan.

Her favorite saying to anyone she met was,
"If I can do this, anyone can."
That's why her experience motivated her to do one other thing. She became the first Debt Free Army member to start training others with the Debt Free Army materials.

She wanted her Christian brothers and sisters to experience this miracle too.

Chapter 9

If You're In A Hole
Stop Digging

Have you ever listened very carefully to the words of the old song "16 Tons" by Tennessee Ernie Ford.

I've updated the song with a few modern lyrics:

> Sixteen cards and what do you get?
>
> Another year older and deeper in debt
>
> Now brother don't you tell me 'cause I already know
>
> It's true what they say that you reap what you sow!

There are way too many believers up to their eyeballs in credit card debt. Every month that you make only the minimum payment on your credit card, <u>you are actually lowering your standard of living</u>.

The first key is an absolute must . . . stop buying stuff on your credit card.   The reason for your purchase doesn't really matter . . . **just STOP NOW.** <u>There will always be some emergency</u>.

Debt isn't something that just happens as you go about your daily routine. Spending habits determine debt. I'm listing five spending habits that will get you into serious financial trouble.

If you have any of these habits, **STOP THEM NOW**, unless you like stress and all the "d" words ... debt, disappointment, discouragement, depression, and disaster (financially speaking, of course).

1. Spending more money than you make

If you only make $1,500 a month, how could you possibly spend $2,000 in a month? This doesn't sound logically possible but it's much easier than you think. In fact, you might be spending more than twice what you make.

Do you dip into your savings, borrow from others, or use credit? These are some primary ways of spending more money than you bring in. You might be able to get away with doing this for a few weeks or even a few months, but soon, your hole-digging spending habits will catch up with you and you'll fall in the hole you dug.

> Spending habits determine debt.
>
> Your hole-digging spending habits will catch up with you and you'll fall in the hole you dug.

One day your savings will be depleted, your credit cards maxed out, and your borrowing will be over. You won't be very popular with anyone except the debt collecting companies who are calling you on a regular basis, saying "Show me the money."

2. Spending phantom money

Spending more money than you make is enabled by a society of credit. <u>Credit allows you to spend money you don't have</u>. You spend money you don't have by using credit cards and taking out loans. When you use these instruments to pay bills and make purchases, you're creating debt. If you can't repay the debt each month, it will continue to grow. And with interest added, it can get out of hand in a hurry.

3. Using credit rather than cash for daily purchases

From your income you should budget cash to make everyday purchases like groceries, gas, clothes, and entertainment. Credit cards give you the ability to pay later for items that you buy now. **It feels like free money because you are putting off the consequences**. But items already consumed lose their luster when it comes time to pay for them. <u>And not paying your credit card bills in full each month is the worst habit of all</u>. If you realized how much that hamburger or new sweater is actually costing, you would be shocked.

4. Using credit when you have cash

Have you ever decided to use your credit card even though you had cash? Why is that? Somehow it feels good to keep that cash for other things and doing so means you feel you have the freedom to spend more.

<u>One of the quickest ways to get into debt is to choose to use credit when you have the cash to make a purchase</u>. People do this with a "something for nothing" type of mind set. They want to buy but they don't want to worry about paying for it

right now. **The convenience of leaving your money in your wallet comes at a cost.** Chances are, if you don't want to pay for it today, you're not going to want to pay for it tomorrow. But the truth is **you will be paying and paying for many tomorrows.**

5. Doing the Debt Shuffle

When you use credit cards to pay off other cards and loans to pay off other loans you're sliding into a dangerous curve. You are spending a lot of time, energy, emotion and money just shuffling your debt around incurring more debt each time you do so.

Balance transfers have transaction fees and most loans have some kind of down payment or origination fee. So when you use debt to pay off debt, you end up worse off than when you began.

> A habit takes about three weeks to become a part of your thought process
> . . . **start today!**

Final Word

It's time for you to stop spending and develop good stewardship habits. A habit takes about three weeks to become a part of your thought process. Start today and in three weeks you can change your financial mind set around to a brighter future.

QUESTIONS:

1. What happens when you only make the minimum
    payment on your credit card each month?

    _____

    _____

    _____

2. What do spending habits determine?

    _____

    _____

3. If you're in a financial hole what should you do?

    _____

    _____

4. What is one of the quickest ways to get into debt?

    _____

    _____

5. How long does it take for a new habit to become a
    part of your thought process?

    _____

    _____

Harold Herring

"My wife and I were at the meeting in Cleveland, Ohio. We [gave an offering] of $200.00.

We were praying that I would receive a favorable decision on my case and we did. I got a check for over $10,000 eleven days later.

We thank God for His loving kindness and mercy! God is always on time!

Thank you, Harold and thank you, Debt Free Army!"

- J.L.D., Cleveland, OH

"We joined the Debt Free Army and within 4 years our house was paid in full."

- L.C.S., Chesapeake, VA

Chapter 10

Worse Than A Snake Bite

With advance apologies to the folks at Animal Planet . . . I hate snakes.

I **could spiritualize it** and tell you that it's **because satan appeared as a snake in the Garden of Eden** . . . but that's **not really true**, at least consciously . . . **I just hate snakes**.

I also **hate when people are charged interest . . . especially the exorbitant interest rates charged by credit card or finance companies. I don't even like it when Christians charge one another interest**. Truthfully, **that practice is unscriptural**.

By now, you're **probably wondering what snakes and interest have in common**. Well, Deuteronomy 23:19-20 tells you the rest of the story.

"19 Thou shalt not lend upon usury to thy brother; usury of money, usury of victuals, usury of any thing that is lent upon usury:

20 Unto a stranger thou mayest lend upon usury; but unto thy brother thou shalt not lend upon usury: that the LORD thy God may bless thee in all that thou settest thine hand to in the land whither thou goest to possess It."

First, the Merriam-Webster Unabridged Collegiate Dictionary defines *usury* as:

"the lending of money with an interest charge for its use *especially* : the lending of money at exorbitant interest rates or an unconscionable or exorbitant rate or amount of interest *specifically* : interest in excess of a legal rate charged to a borrower."

Second, in Deuteronomy 23:19 there are two different Hebrew words translated for the word *usury*.

"Thou shalt not lend upon usury [5391] to thy brother; usury [5392] of money, usury [5392] of victuals, usury [5392] of any thing that is lent upon usury." [5391]

In verse 19, the word usury is listed **five times but there are two different meanings in the Hebrew that are translated as *usury*.**

The second, third and fourth times the word usury is used . . . it's the Hebrew word **neshek** (H5392) which means **"interest on debt**." This use of the word is found **12 times in 10 verses in the Hebrew concordance of the King James Version of the Bible**.

I'm not going to list all ten verses for you to read . . . but they have some pretty strong language about charging interest to a fellow believer.

Proverbs 28:8 says:

"He that by usury and unjust gain increaseth his substance, he shall gather it for him that will pity the poor."

The Amplified Bible translation says:

"He who by charging excessive interest and who by unjust efforts to get gain increases his material possession gathers it for him [to spend] who is kind and generous to the poor."

All of the scriptures using the Hebrew word *neshek* are very clear but none more so than **Ezekiel 22:12** in the Amplified Bible:

"In you they have accepted bribes to shed blood; you have taken [forbidden] interest and [percentage of] increase, and you have greedily gained from your neighbors by oppression and extortion and have forgotten Me, says the Lord God."

The other verses using the same Hebrew word for *interest* are: Exodus 22:25; Leviticus 25:36; Leviticus 25:37; Psalm 15:5; and Ezekiel 18: 8, 13, 17. In your personal Bible study time I encourage you to look up these verses for further confirmation.

> God's plan is for us to provide for one another.

The other Hebrew word used in Deuteronomy 23:19 is *nashak* (H5391) which is the first and last usage of *usury*. According to the Strong's Dictionary of Words, *nashak* means **"to strike with a sting like a serpent; bite; to oppress with interest on a loan."**

Nashak is used <u>16 times in 14 verses in the Hebrew concordance of the King James Version of the Bible</u>. In every single instance the verses **refer to being bitten by snakes with deadly consequences**.

For instance, Numbers 21:6 in the Amplified Bible says:

"Then the Lord sent fiery (burning) serpents among the people; and they bit the people, and many Israelites died."

Bite is translated from *nashak* the same Hebrew word used for *usury* or *interest.*

When it comes to interest and the sting . . . the bite of debt . . . then Habakkuh 2:7 in the Amplified Bible tells it like it is:

"Shall [your debtors] not rise up suddenly who shall bite you, exacting usury of you, and those awake who will vex you [toss you to and fro and make you tremble violently]? Then you will be booty for them."

"Make you tremble violently" sounds to me like what happens when someone is bitten by the sting of debt. If you're in debt or have ever been in debt, then you can understand the feelings described in verse 7.

When the balances on your **credit cards and other debts never seem to get any smaller even though you're making your payments on time** . . . that is the sting of debt.

When you're facing foreclosure or eviction . . . debt has slithered up and taken a bite out of your peace and happiness.

The bite and sting of the interest serpent can literally sneak up on you unnoticed <u>until it sinks its fangs filled with debtor poison into your finances</u>.

The word *nashak* is also used in the following verses: Genesis 49:17; Numbers 21:8, 9; Numbers 21:9; Deuteronomy 23:20; Proverbs 23:32; Ecclesiastes10:8, 11; Jeremiah 8:17; Amos 5:19, Amos 9:3, and Micah 3:5.

The law referred to in Deuteronomy 23:19-20 was given to the **Israelites not necessarily to forbid all interest but to protect and provide for the poor.** In Bible times, **no one was to borrow money unless they were facing a totally desperate situation. To charge another Israelite interest would be viewed as kicking someone when they were down.**

The **model for compassion** that's demonstrated throughout the scriptures is in **taking care of our own.** Not the government. Not the credit card company charging them 18% interest and higher.

God's plan is for us to provide for one another. That was the practice of the New Testament Church in the Book of Acts.

> Going to church doesn't make you a Christian any more than walking into McDonalds makes you a Big Mac.

Now I feel prompted to say that the scripture also teaches . . . **that if you don't work, you don't eat.** That is **unless someone is not capable of working**.

We're to **help those who have shown themselves faithful and are truly needy**.

One more thing . . . **there are people who go to church but that doesn't make them a brother or sister in the Lord.** Going to church doesn't make you a Christian any more than walking into McDonalds makes you a Big Mac. **Walking out the Christian life in daily living reveals the true nature of the spirit in a person.**

Use wisdom and discernment . . . that's why God gives to you freely of both.

I think it's fair to say that **the law encouraged giving more than it did lending**.

Consider the words found in **Luke 6:35** in the Amplified Bible:

"But love your enemies and be kind and do good [doing favors so that someone derives benefit from them] and lend, expecting and hoping for nothing in return but considering nothing as lost and despairing of no one; and then your recompense (your reward) will be great (rich, strong, intense, and abundant), and you will be sons of the Most High, for He is kind and charitable and good to the ungrateful and the selfish and wicked."

Let's go a little further and consider the words found in **Deuteronomy 23:20** in the Message Bible.

"Don't charge interest to your kinsmen on any loan: not for money or food or clothing or anything else that could earn interest. You may charge foreigners interest, but you may not charge your brothers interest; that way God, your God, will bless all the work that you take up and the land that you are entering to possess.."

According to this passage it's okay to charge foreigners interest . . . those outside of the Body of Christ . . . but not at exorbitant rates.

Are you ready to get excited . . . let's review the last phrase in verse 20:

". . .God, your God, will bless all the work that you take up in the land that you are entering to possess."

Hallelujah. God will bless ALL the work that you take up.

Whatever your hands find to do will be blessed.

God is not only going to bless what you do . . . He's going to bless you wherever you go.

1. What are two things I hate?

   _____

2. List the two Hebrew words used in the Miriam-Webster's dictionary definition of the word *usury*.

   _____

   _____

3. What is defined as the sting of debt?

   _____

4. What was the practice of the New Testament Church in the Book of Acts and God's plan for us?

   _____

   _____

   _____

5. According to Luke 6:35, by loving your enemies and giving without the expectation of recompense, how will men be rewarded?

   _____

   _____

6. God honors a giving heart. When was the last time you remember giving unselfishly to someone and feeling the blessings of God in your life? Even if the sum was small or the deed minute, did the Lord bless your efforts?

   _____

   _____

   _____

   _____

Chapter 11

The Hidden Consequences Of Debt

We've determined that debt is evil . . . that creditors want you as a booty call and that interest is worst than a snake bite.

As we begin our discussion of the hidden consequences of debt I'm going to make a **profound statement** . . . one I'm sure you've never said or even thought of.

Men and women think differently.

(Smiling) and thankful to God women are different than men. **Some of the differences are obvious (and delightfully so)** and **some are hidden** but I'm going to get to that part later so stay with me for a little while.

God used 2 Kings 4:1 to prompt me to write about "The Hidden Consequences of Debt." Without question, I've taught **this passage of scripture well over 1,000 times over the years and that's no exaggeration**.

However, God recently stirred a fresh revelation in me to share with you in this book.

"Now there cried a certain woman of the wives of the sons of the prophets unto Elisha, saying, Thy servant my husband is dead; and thou knowest that thy servant did fear the

LORD: and the creditor is come to take unto him my two sons to be bondmen."

Here's the revelation. **Men and women look at debt differently.**

Some men view debt as a smart business tool.

Some men view debt as **a necessary evil to get the toys they want**.

Some men view debt as **no big deal as there is always tomorrow's paychec**k.

Some men view debt **with no thought or plan to pay it off**.

As the late Dr. Edwin Louis Cole used to teach: **men are headliners** . . . they're not so concerned about the details.

Some years ago, I read somewhere . . . that there are <u>three differences between men and women when it comes to money</u>.

They have:

Different fears . . . **no matter how much money a husband makes even with the total of their two incomes** . . . there is **always a concern that it's not enough as far as the wife is concerned**. These feelings are **fueled by the three "Ds"** that concern most women. They are: **debt, divorce, and death**. I'll talk more about this later.

Men tend to fear specific events . . . getting fired, or laid off, or injured. A man's concerns are more black and white.

<u>Different approaches</u> . . . women tend to be **better**

planners and more logical in their financial thinking whereas a man's approach to finances is <u>simply talking with his best friend</u> or maybe a financial planner or two. That's good enough for him.

I mentioned earlier that Dr. Cole said men are headliners. He described **women as fine printers** . . . they want to know all the details. **A man is more apt to take another man's word that the contract he's about to sign is okay** . . . **but a woman is going to ask questions**.

<u>Different goals</u> . . . women typically **see retirement as a time to start a business, home-based or otherwise**. Whereas, most men just want to kick back . . . play golf, fish, <u>maybe travel (if it's to the right places)</u> and **basically do nothing that further financially solidifies their later years**.

I know you're wondering what happened to the widow in 2 Kings but stay with me . . . I'm getting there.

Earlier, I mention the three "Ds" . . . **debt, divorce, and death** that are a major concern to most women. I want to explore these a little further.

For most women, **debt is a security issue**.

First, let's look at debt.

Debt without a **plan to pay it off** in a timely manner **can jeopardize the home** and well-being of the family. For most every woman and especially mothers . . . **this is totally unacceptable**.

My fine wife, Bev, has ALWAYS hated debt. In the early years of our marriage I **misinterpreted her concern and just rationalized that she was "tight."**

(Personal Note)—she still **is "tight" but in the popular jargon** used to mean **"fine."** **But back then she was tight when it came to spending money.**

In fact, I used to tell my friends that if the **dictionary had pictures** . . . my fine wife's photo would be placed beside the word "tight."

However, over the years **I've gotten smarter** . . . thanks to **the Holy Spirit, the school of hard knocks, and my fine wife.**

Most women are natural planners . . . so they have **trouble seeing how debt, especially excessive debt, fits into any picture of success.**

Women are also concerned about divorce . . . at any time . . . but especially when there is debt involved.

I can't begin to tell you the **horror stories** I've heard **about some sinful slacker husband** who has **run up the debts** and then **bailed on his wife and children** . . . leaving them to survive any way they can.

I could tell you story after story about **families losing homes**, mothers working two and three jobs and **children** placed in peril because of the debt left behind during a divorce.

Then, **women are also concerned about death**.

In the past, many women have been left to deal with debt after the divorce or death of a spouse like the widow in 2 Kings.

The woman's husband died. The scripture doesn't say **how he died** but I believe it was because of the stress of debt.

We **know he was in debt** because the Word says that the creditors were coming to take her two sons because of the debts.

The Message Bible translation of 2 Kings 4:1 says:

". . . And now the man to whom he was in debt is on his way to collect by taking my two children as slaves."

Not only had this woman lost her husband to death . . . **she was now about to lose her two sons to debt**.

In biblical times, if a **woman wasn't married or didn't have sons to provide for her** . . . she **found survival very difficult at best**.

Her husband had left her with **an enormous debt and no visible way of repaying it** . . . now she was going to lose her sons.

No doubt before the prophet died, he **never thought he'd be putting his family in such jeopardy when he got into all that debt**. In his mind, he probably thought that he'd be around for years and have the debt paid off long before his **family experienced any consequences**.

The widow woman and her sons were experiencing the hidden consequences of debt.

It is **not negative or fatalistic thinking on behalf of a married woman to think of the consequences** she and her family may face in the event of death.

I recommend that every woman, and man for that matter, **begin educating themselves on finances if they haven't already**. I consider it absolutely necessary that you have a plan to get out of debt.

Sadly, **some women never learn about financial matters because their husband doesn't want them to know about money and debt. If you're married to one of those men who won't share finances with you** . . . **then learn on your own.**

There is **more teaching on finances and getting out of debt now than ever before in our history.** The Internet has a lot of free information and teaching. May I suggest you start at www.debtfreearmy.org.

> Educate yourself now . . . so you can avoid the hidden consequence of debt.

The library is also a great resource since there's **no charge for borrowing books, CDs or DVDs.**

Let me be clear . . . **for a woman not to educate herself about finances because of her husband's attitude is just an excuse and sadly, one day she may come to regret that decision.** And by the way, <u>**don't assume that he's smarter than you are when it comes to financial matters**</u>.

Don't let your family end up like the prophet's widow . . . **needing a miracle to survive. Educate yourself now** . . . **so you can avoid the hidden consequence of debt.**

Debt Determines Your Environment

QUESTIONS:

1. What verse describes the "hidden consequences of debt?"

   _____

2. Men and women look at debt differently. How do men view debt?

   _____
   _____
   _____

3. What are the three differences between a man and woman's views on debt?

   _____
   _____
   _____

4. What did the late Dr. Edwin Louis Cole mean by the statement "men are head-liners?"

   _____

   What about the statement that "women are fineprinters?"

   _____

5. Why do some happily married women never learn about the finances of the household?

   _____
   _____

6. Where are some good places to begin looking for information?

   _____
   _____
   www._____.org

91

"I attended your meeting and purchased one of your products. Since then we have purchased a new 2,500 square foot home and are moving ahead to get completely out of debt.

God instructed me to put together a small workshop and share the things I have learned that has helped us get a hold of our finances.

I look forward to attending your next meeting."

- SG, Virginia Beach, VA

"I am so blessed and the Lord continues to bless me. I sent a $100 to the Debt Free Army and a month later I won a $1000 in a contest at work."

- P.S., Broadlands, VA

Chapter 12

The Wages Of Debt Is Death

"For the wages of sin is death. . ."

In the Strong's Concordance the word *wages* is the Greek word *opsōnion* (G3800) and it means: **"a soldier's pay, allowance; that part of the soldier's support given in place of pay [i.e. rations] and the money in which he is paid."**

The word *sin* in Romans 6:23 is the Greek word *hamartia* (G266) and it's defined as: **"that which is done wrong, sin, an offence, a violation of the divine law in thought or in act."**

In Strong's the word *death* is the Greek word *thanatos* (G2288) and it means: **"that separation (whether natural or violent) of the soul and the body by which the life on earth is ended."**

Death is also defined in Strong's as: "in the widest sense, death comprising all the miseries arising from sin, as well physical death **as the loss of a life consecrated to God and blessed in him on earth**, to be followed by wretchedness in hell."

So the wages of sin . . . **what you're paid when you do wrong, to violate the Word of God in thought and deed**

will result in the loss of a life blessed in him on the earth.

Here are several scriptures the Lord brought to my attention as I was writing these words.

Matthew 6:12 in the Amplified Bible says:

"And forgive us our debts, as we also have forgiven (left, remitted, and let go of the debts, and have given up resentment against) our debtors."

In the Strong's Concordance the word *debts* is the Greek word "G3783 – *opheilēma* and it means: **"that which is owed" or "that which is justly or legally due, a debt."**

So the scripture is very clear to me . . . it you have debts, then you need to be forgiven of those debts.

> "Don't run up debts, except for the huge debt of love you owe each other."
> Romans 13:8
> The Message Bible

The scripture also tells us to keep out of debt. The Amplified Bible version of Romans 13:8 amplifies the meaning of each Greek word used giving us a broader translation:

*"Keep out of **debt** and owe no man anything, except to love one another; for he who loves his neighbor [who practices loving others] has fulfilled the Law [relating to one's fellowmen, meeting all its requirements]."*

The Message Bible is also quite clear:

"Don't run up debts, except for the huge debt of love you

owe each other."

There are consequences to debt.

Matthew 18:25 in the New Living Translation says:

"He couldn't pay, so his master ordered that he be sold—along with his wife, his children, and everything he owned—to pay the debt."

2 Kings 4:1 in the Message Bible says:

"One day the wife of a man from the guild of prophets called out to Elisha, "Your servant my husband is dead. You well know what a good man he was, devoted to God. And now <u>the man to whom he was in debt is on his way to collect by taking my two children as slaves</u>."

We can be "good" as the prophet described in 2 Kings but what happens if you don't obey God . . . including piling up bad debts?

Ezekiel 18:10 in the Message Bible says:

"But if this person has a child who turns violent and murders and goes off and does any of these things, even though the parent has done none of them— eats at the pagan shrines, seduces his neighbor's spouse, bullies the weak, steals, <u>piles up bad debts</u>, admires idols, commits outrageous obscenities, exploits the poor "—do you think this person, the child, will live? Not a chance! Because he's done all these vile things, he'll die. And his death will be his own fault."

Finally, let's consider **what happens when you are debt free and walk in God's will for your life**.

Ezekiel 18:5 in the Message Bible says:

"Imagine a person who lives well, treating others fairly, keeping good relationships— doesn't eat at the pagan shrines, doesn't worship the idols so popular in Israel, doesn't seduce a neighbor's spouse, doesn't indulge in casual sex, doesn't bully anyone, <u>doesn't pile up bad debts</u>, doesn't steal, doesn't refuse food to the hungry, doesn't refuse clothing to the ill-clad, doesn't exploit the poor, doesn't live by impulse and greed, doesn't treat one person better than another, But lives by my statutes and faithfully honors and obeys my laws. This person who lives upright and well shall live a full and true life. Decree of God, the Master."

I don't think you'll die and go to hell if you're in debt.

I just think you'll feel like you're already living in hell because your life is not your own.

The wages of debt is death to your hope and dreams.

Stay with me now . . . **I don't think you'll die and go to hell if you're in debt**. I just think **<u>you'll feel like you're already living in hell because your life is not your own</u>**. Your creditors control your life . . . they take away your personal freedom . . . They take away your ability to enjoy peace of mind . . . to spend two weeks on the mission field if you want to . . . and **sow big into the kingdom of God**.

Make no mistake . . . **your creditors (who feel like financial blood suckers) will use debt to suck the very life out of you** . . . <u>they'll clean you out quicker than any vampire ever could</u>.

If you're in debt . . . create a plan to get out of debt. **Hang**

around with people who are committed to establishing their own financial independence.

The wages of debt is death to your hope and dreams.

Never give the enemy or your creditors that kind of control over your life.

Practice the wisdom found in Romans 13:8 in the Message Bible:

> *"Don't run up debts, except for the huge debt of love you owe each other."*

QUESTIONS:

1. According to Strong's Concordance what word is defined as "that separation (whether natural or violent) of the soul and the body by which the life on earth is ended."

    _____

2. What does the Bible tell us to do regarding debt, in Romans 13:8?

    _____

    _____

3. Name one of the biblical examples of the consequences of debt.

    _____

    _____

4. If you are in debt, what kind of people should you surround yourself with?

    _____

    _____

    _____

5. What are the wages of debt? What are the advantages of being out of debt?

    _____

    _____

    _____

    _____

    _____

Chapter 13

Good Debt
Bad Debt

I have read all 800,000 words in the 66 chapters of the Bible from Genesis 1:1 to Revelation 22:21.

In fact, I've read the Bible through a number of times but I have never once seen where the Bible says that debt is good. It's just not in the book.

Truthfully, **the fact that the scripture has nothing positive to say about debt should give us pause, if not concern, about its potential for evil**.

Scripturally speaking, debt in and of itself, is not a sin. If it were a sin, no doubt the Word would have discussed the wages of debt just as it does the wages of sin.

While being in debt may not be a sin . . . as far as lenders and borrowers go . . . we are to be on the lending side.

Deuteronomy 15:6 in the Amplified Bible says:

"When the Lord your God blesses you as He promised you, then you shall lend to many nations, but you shall not borrow; and you shall rule over many nations, but they shall not rule over you."

The scripture says *"you shall not borrow."* That statement is pretty clear to me. Do not borrow.

There are some who talk about debt as being good and bad. Let's talk a look at the various kinds of debt . . . and see whether it's good or bad.

There are five kinds of debt . . . business, consumer, credit card, investment and mortgage.

Consumer and credit card debt are the result of the flesh wanting something . . . to make a person feel better about himself or better than somebody else. I won't say this is an absolute fact . . .but pretty close to it. <u>Many people buy stuff to impress their friends and family or just to make themselves feel better</u>.

James 1:13 says:

"But every man is tempted, when he is drawn away of his own lust, and enticed."

James 4:3 says:

"Ye ask, and receive not, because ye ask amiss, that ye may consume it upon your lusts."

Do you find it interesting that James 4:3 uses the word *"consume?"*

There was a time when people wanted to keep up with the Jones. However, that's not necessary anymore because the Joneses have already declared Chapter 13 bankruptcy.

The kind of wants or lusts that birth consumer and credit card debt includes: vacations, big-ticket items such as electronics and appliances; fancy cars, entertainment; furniture; aesthetic home improvement; and the list could go on and on. They are wants, not needs, and people will go in debt to have them.

There is an amazing parallel to the rise of advertising in this country and the upward spiral of debt. The media and its advertisers create a false impression and conception of what the good life really is.

<u>**The Pied Pipers of wants and lusts play a hypnotic message that has caused millions and millions of consumers to swallow the bait of wants** . . . **hook, line and sinker.**</u>

The invention of credit card debt has taken place in the past 50 years. **Total credit card debt in this country was nearly $1 TRILLION dollars through mid 2011** *(Visit creditcard.com for the latest statistics on credit card usage).* The evolution of credit card debt and the strangle hold it has on millions of Americans is frightening.

> "You will lose your self-respect and end up in debt to some cruel person for the rest of your life."
> - Proverbs 5:9 CEV

So the bottom line and this is not an absolute . . . but pretty close to it . . . <u>consumer and credit card debt is designed to continually take advantage of the personal weaknesses of the average American.</u>

We're told to be good consumers. I find it interesting that Dictionary.Com defines *consume* as: **"to destroy or expend by use; use up; to spend (money, time, etc.) wastefully."**

The American Heritage Dictionary defines *consume*: **"to waste, to squander."**

Millions upon millions of dollars are spent to lure people into the lifestyle of debt as they pursue what Madison Avenue advertisers and Hollywood personalities define as the good life.

They want you to believe that as long as you're getting what you want . . . debt is okay. No, it's not. It is actually self defeating and in the end, quite humiliating.

Proverbs 22:7 in the Contemporary English Version says:

"The poor are ruled by the rich, and those who borrow are slaves of moneylenders."

Proverbs 5:9 also in the Contemporary English Version says:

"You will lose your self-respect and end up in debt to some cruel person for the rest of your life."

I think we can agree that consumer and credit card debt are evil.

You may be asking . . . what is generally considered good debt?

Most people consider a home mortgage to be good debt. It is true that mortgage debt is a financial liability but it can be an offsetting asset. That's assuming your home is located in an area where property values are appreciating . . . **and** you have a plan to pay the mortgage off rapidly without wasting a significant amount of your income on interest.

However, there are significant numbers of people in the past year that have found home ownership to be anything but good debt. The plummeting of property values, the loss of jobs, the evaporation of investment portfolios, the increase in foreclosures are all factors that have affected whether home ownership is good debt.

Bottom line . . . **you've got to have a workable plan** . . . otherwise, in an economic downturn such as the one we're facing right now . . . you can lose that asset which you thought was a good investment of your resources.

We have written strategies to pay off your mortgage in seven years or less . . . that's the only way it's a good debt . . . when it's paid off. At that point you can begin to invest your money in other areas.

Second, some people consider higher education a good debt. To the extent that a college degree increases your value in the marketplace resulting in higher compensation . . . it is good. However, student loans are the closest thing there is to financial slavery.

These loans are easy to get into but difficult to pay off. Even technical schools and colleges are now charging students exorbitant rates for their education. Sadly, the primary focus of many of the so-called colleges springing up around the country is the bottom line . . . making a huge profit.

Third, business and investment debt can be good; however, you need to exercise caution and planning.

Do your homework before buying. <u>Do not take out a home equity loan or amass a pile of credit card debt to take advantage of what you learned at a weekend seminar on real estate investing, profiting on foreclosures or making it big in the stock market</u>. Sadly, you need to realize the people doing the seminars are making most of their money on the people who pay to attend the seminars and buy their products.

Let's summarize. . .

Debt is bad for some people simply because. they can't handle credit.

Debt is bad for some people simply because they can't handle credit. They don't have the discipline to make wise decisions . . . the knowledge to understand the consequences of debt . . . or the personal desire to do whatever is necessary to increase their understanding of matters financial.

I should not need to say this when writing to a primarily Christian audience but I feel led to do so . . . incurring debt with no intention of repaying it is morally and scripturally wrong.

Debt is bad if it creates strife in your family . . . prohibits you from doing the things that the scripture clearly instructs you to do . . . requires you to make decisions based on the world instead of the Word.

The only way debt is ever good . . . is if there is an offsetting asset . . . and you have a plan to pay the debt off rapidly . . . not someday . . . but now.

Too many people in the world, either give up hope completely or they fall into the "**someday syndrome.**"

"Someday, things will get better."

"Someday, I'm going to have money."

"Someday, I won't have to work like this."

"Someday, I'm going to get out of debt."

"Someday, I'll start giving the way I really want to."

I have news for you . . . someday is TODAY . . . right now . . . this is the day for you to determine there is going to be an immediate change in your finances . . . you'll stop buying what you want and only what you need. Today, you're creating a plan to get out of debt RAPIDLY.

When your someday becomes today . . . then the words of Job 41:11 in the Contemporary English Version will become a reality in your life.

"I am in command of the world and in debt to no one."

You will also become an example of Romans 13:8 in the Amplified Bible which says:

"Keep out of debt and owe no man anything, except to love one another; for he who loves his neighbor [who practices loving others] has fulfilled the Law [relating to one's fellow men, meeting all its requirements]."

QUESTIONS:

1. How many words and chapters are in the Bible?

   _____

2. The fact that the Bible does not speak positively about debt is an indicator that debt is . . .

   _____

3. What are the five different types of debt?

   _____
   _____
   _____
   _____
   _____

4. There is an amazing parallel to the rise of advertising in this country and the upward spiral of

   _____
   .

5. Consumer and credit card debt is designed to continually take advantage of whom?

   _____

6. What is the closest thing to financial slavery in today's world? _____

7. When there is an offsetting asset and you plan to pay the debt off rapidly (immediately), then debt can be considered good. Have you encountered bad debt? _____

   How did the situation change when you realized you had bad debt?

   _____
   _____
   _____

Chapter 14

What Does Debt Free Mean?

What does "debt free" really mean?

In frequent conversations at my seminars I will invariably have someone tell me that they're debt free, except for their mortgage.

I've had others tell me they're debt free except for this bill or that bill . . . generally student loans fall into the equation.

If you go to google.com and type in the words "debt free" your page will be filled with links to various debt consolidation companies.

I remember traveling in Detroit about ten years ago on the way to a Debt Free Rally. My taxi drove past a finance company that had a big sign in the window. It read:

"Now You Can Borrow Enough Money To Be Debt Free."

I could hardly believe my eyes. That's not the definition of being debt free but they evidently felt like there would be enough people who would believe it or they wouldn't have put it in their window.

For some "debt free" means the absence of any financial liabilities. My mentor, Brother John Avanzini, says that being "debt free" means that you never have to say "no" to God when He tells you to give.

For me, the scriptural answer is clear and it's found in Romans 13:8:

"Owe no man anything, but to love one another: for he that loveth another hath fulfilled the law."

I've heard it taught that Romans 13:8 isn't referring to financial debt but rather a "debt" of love. Excuse me for being direct . . . but that's just goofy theology.

The Amplified Bible Translation of Romans 13:8 says:

"Keep out of debt and owe no man anything, except to love one another; for he who loves his neighbor [who practices loving others] has fulfilled the Law [relating to one's fellowmen, meeting all its requirements]."

The Message Bible translates the verse as:

"Don't run up debts, except for the huge debt of love you owe each other. When you love others, you complete what the law has been after all along."

However, let's go further in our research of the word *owe* as found in Romans 13:8.

First, what is the Strong's Concordance definition of owe? A little research will reveal that the word *owe* in the Greek is the word *opheilo* (G3784) and it means: "to owe money, be in debt for."

The Greek word for *owe* (G3784) appears 36 times in 35 verses of the Bible between Matthew 18:28 and 3 John 1:8. The meaning is the same in every verse.

Second, what is the secular dictionary definition of owe?

According to Webster's Revised Unabridged Dictionary the word *debt* means: "That which is due from one person to another, whether money, goods, or services; that which one person is bound to pay to another, or to perform for his benefit; thing owed; obligation; liability."

Third, it's important to consider what the verse prior (Romans 13:7 CEV) has to say:

"Pay all that you owe, whether it is taxes and fees or respect and honor."

The Message Bible translation of verse 7 says:

"Fulfill your obligations as a citizen. Pay your taxes, pay your bills, respect your leaders."

But let's go a little further with Romans 13:8.

"Owe no man anything, but to love one another: for he that loveth another hath fulfilled the law."

The two words *no man* is the Greek word "*mēdeis*" (G3367) and it means: "nobody; no one, nothing."

It is interesting to note that the Greek word for *anything* is the same Greek word that is used for *no man*.

The first part of this verse is saying, "Do not be in debt to anybody for anything."

Debt free means just that . . . free of debts of any kind other than monthly utilities. PERIOD. PARAGRAPH.

QUESTIONS:

1. Is a person debt free if they borrow the amount
    they are in debt from a friend, neighbor, or no-
    interest for five years loan from a banking
    institution?

    _____

2. How did Brother John Avanzini define debt free?

    _____
    _____
    _____

3. What is the Strong's Concordance definition of the
    word *owe*?

    _____
    _____
    _____

4. How does Webster's dictionary define the word
    owe?

    _____
    _____
    _____

5. Does the Bible condone debt so long as it is debt
    acquired for a good reason like buying a new car
    or owning an iPad? _____

6. The Greek word for *anything* means the same as
    which other Greek word?

    _____
    _____
    _____

Chapter 15

Break The Power
Of Debt Now

You must defeat, destroy and eliminate the power of the spirit of debt and lack out of your life FOREVER.

Is that possible? Let's see what the Word of God has to say about it.

". . . devils are subject unto us through thy name."
        Luke 10:17

Debt is a spirit and a spiritual battle. All spirits must leave when they are commanded to do so in the strong name of Jesus.

"Behold, I give unto you power to tread on serpents and scorpions, and over all the power of the enemy and nothing shall by any means hurt you."
        Luke 10:19

The first *power* used in this scripture is the Greek Word *exousia* (G1849) in Strong's Concordance and it means "the power of authority (influence) and of right (privilege)."

The second *power* used in this scripture is the Greek Word *dynamis* (G1411) and it means "strength, power and ability."

So what this scripture is saying is as the children of the most

111

high God, we have all authority over all the abilities of the enemy and nothing can by any means hurt us! Debt can never hurt you once you take authority over it.

"And whatsoever ye shall ask in my name that will I do, that the Father may be glorified in the Son."
John 14:13

God has given us power in the spirit world. However, before any problem that arises from demon spirits can be solved, **the chief spirit must be dealt with**.

". . . how can one enter into a strong man's house, and spoil his goods, except he first bind the strong man? And then he will spoil the house."
Matthew 12:29

Debt has become a strong man that is holding way too many Christians captive.

"and if satan rise up against himself, and be divided, he cannot stand, but hath an end. No man can enter into a strong man's house, and spoil his goods, except he first bind the strongman; then he will spoil his house."
Mark 3:26-27

A study of the scripture shows us . . . there is a spirit of debt. He is as subtle as a mistress. I encourage you to read my blog about how the prostitute in Proverbs 6 & 7 is like the sultry spirit of debt . . . enticing your eyes with her goods and leading you down the path of destruction.

Every good gift comes down from the Father (James 1:7). Debt is an evil mistress who entices her victims into a tangled web that is difficult to get out of without the power of God. Once a person's eyes are opened and the evil exposed, debt does not have its lure.

This spirit has influenced the lost, but it has **also driven most of the Christian world into a lifestyle of debt**. **The power of the spirit of debt must be broken before you or anyone else can receive the full prosperity of God**.

In Debt Free rallies, seminars and church services around the world, I have **asked people to either bring their bills to the meeting or hold up a piece of paper representing their bills**. I have everyone pray with me in the precious and powerful place of agreement asking God to break the power of the spirit of debt out of their lives forever. **I then rebuke the spirit of debt and command it to go out of every household represented by an uplifted hand**.

Every time God allows me to command the spirit of debt to leave there is <u>always a fresh anointing for those who are willing to step out of their comfort zone and extend their faith</u>.

I can tell you **on the authority of the Word that breaking the power of the spirit of debt is not nearly as hard as the devil would have you believe**. However, <u>to succeed, you must take several definite steps</u>. Please prayerfully read the following list.

1. You must sit down and list all the bills you owe. <u>This accounting must be done before you can launch a proper plan of attack against the havoc created by the spirit of debt in your personal finances</u>. This is not just a secular approach to your problem. It is prescribed by the Lord Himself.

"For which of you, intending to build a tower, sitteth not down first, and counteth the cost, whether he have sufficient to finish it."
        Luke 14:28

Count the cost the spirit of debt has brought to your life. Recognize that he has been the motivating force behind your bills. When you have the whole picture clearly outlined before you, **ask God for the specific financial miracles you need to free you from the bondage of your debt**.

> If you are not acknowledging financial miracles, they will cease.

Remember to be thankful for any progress you make in debt reduction.

Your first financial miracle may be very small, but acknowledge that it has come from God. **If you are not acknowledging financial miracles, they will cease. Be sure to let principalities and powers know that it is not your last financial miracle**. There will be many more.

". . . faith is the substance of things hoped for. . ."
        Hebrews 11:1

2. If at all possible, you should have a relationship with a good local church. This is important because giving your tithes into good ground is necessary to keep the windows of heaven open over your finances. You cannot expect to reap financial miracles unless the windows of heaven are open over your life. It also rebukes the devourer from coming against the seed you sow into God's Kingdom. You can expect great harvests.

"Bring ye all the tithes into the storehouse, that there may be meat in mine house, and prove me now herewith, saith the Lord of hosts, if I will not open the windows of heaven, and pour you out a blessing, that there shall not be room enough to receive it.

11And I will rebuke the devourer for your sakes, and he

shall not destroy the fruits of your ground; neither shall your vine cast her fruit before the time in the field, saith the LORD of hosts."
Malachi 3:10, 11

3. It is also necessary to associate yourself with some good-ground ministries such as a Christian television station or network, a good Bible teacher, or an evangelist. The reason this relationship is necessary is that you will need a good place to give your offerings. Your offerings will provide God with the measure He needs to pour out your financial blessings. (Luke 6:38; 2 Corinthians 9:6)

4. The strong man must be bound.

". . . how can one enter into a strong man's house, and spoil his goods, except he first bind the strong man?"
Matthew 12:29

<u>**You must speak specifically to the strong man (the spirit of debt)**</u>. <u>Bind him from any further interference in your finances</u>. To put it plainly, he must release his hold on your money. Be sure you **do this in the strong name of Jesus, for His name is infinitely stronger than the spirit of debt**.

"That at the name of Jesus every knee should bow, of the things in heaven, and things in earth, and things under the earth."
Philippians 2:10

Don't be afraid when you speak to the spirit of debt. It is the spirit of debt who must be afraid. <u>You have someone bigger and stronger within you than anything the devil has</u>.

". . . greater is he that is in you, than he that is in the world."
1 John 4:4

5. Now lift up your bills before the Lord, and repeat this prayer. Say it out loud.

"Heavenly Father, I know You love and care for me, spirit, soul, and body. Lord, I have bills and they are a hindrance to me because they keep me from giving to You the way I really want to. Lord, I believe what Harold Herring taught me about the spirit of debt is true. I believe what the Word of God says, that You are a debt-canceling God. I believe that if You canceled debt for the widow and her two sons or anyone else, You will do it for me. I believe You are concerned about my bills and You have given me the authority to eliminate them from my life. Lord, I speak that in the strong name of Jesus, the spirit of debt and lack are broken from my life. I speak that it is broken at the root so that it will never return again. I also ask You for the supernatural elimination and cancellation of my debts. Father, I believe that in joining my faith together with this man of God something special is being released into my life. I thank You that You have given me authority over the entire spirit world as stated in 1 John 1:8.

"Right now, I boldly speak to the chief spirit, the spirit of debt that has been sent by the devil. In the strong name of Jesus, I declare you bound. I break your hold on my life and on my finances! Spirit of debt, you can no longer operate in my life! In the strong name of Jesus you are firmly bound, and I am loosed from your power over me!

"Father God, part the heavens for me. This is the confidence I have . . . I have asked in accordance with Your will so I know I have the petitions I have placed before You today (1John 5:4;14). The foul spirit of debt has been bound and defeated.

"I now speak to the East, the West, the North, and the South that the ministering angels of God come forth and begin to release the abundance of God into my life (Psalm 103:20). I boldly speak that miracles begin to take place in my finances right now. In the strong name of Jesus, I accept my financial breakthrough and I praise You, Father, that the spirit of debt and lack has been broken out of my life forever.

"Lord, I give You the glory for the financial miracles being released into my life this day, right now . . . in Jesus' name. Amen."

Say It Out Loud!

Now, say it out loud. **"The power of the spirit of debt and lack has been broken from my life."** Say it until it rings in the devil's ears. Debt has controlled your finances for the last time.

> Don't be afraid when you speak to the spirit of debt.

If you are married, tell your spouse that the spirit of debt and lack has been broken from your lives. **If you are single, tell the next person you meet or a prayer partner that the spirit of debt has been broken off your life.** Join together in proclaiming your financial victory.

"If the Son therefore, shall make you free, ye shall be free indeed."
        John 8:36

Is It That Easy?

Yes, it's that easy to break the power of the spirit of debt and lack out of your life. It was that easy once you made the decision to get saved, it's that easy to bind and eliminate the spirit of debt from your life FOREVER. God's Word backs you up!

117

A Word of Caution

The spirit of debt and lack has been broken out of your life but **it's critical that you stop doing that which got you into debt in the first place**. Because if you continue that kind of spending then **debt will come back and bring seven of his buddies with him and your debt will be worse than ever before**.

"43 When the unclean spirit is gone out of a man, he walketh through dry places, seeking rest, and findeth none.

44 Then he saith, I will return into my house from whence I came out; and when he is come, he findeth it empty, swept, and garnished.

45 Then goeth he, and taketh with himself seven other spirits more wicked than himself, and they enter in and dwell there: and the last state of that man is worse than the first. Even so shall it be also unto this wicked generation."
Matthew 12:43-45

Matthew 12:43-45 in the Message Bible says it this way:

"When a defiling evil spirit is expelled from someone, it drifts along through the desert looking for an oasis, some unsuspecting soul it can bedevil. When it doesn't find anyone, it says, 'I'll go back to my old haunt.' On return it finds the person spotlessly clean, but vacant. It then runs out and rounds up seven other spirits more evil than itself and they all move in, whooping it up. That person ends up far worse off than if he'd never gotten cleaned up in the first place.

"That's what this generation is like: You may think you have cleaned out the junk from your lives and gotten ready for God, but you weren't hospitable to my kingdom message,

and now all the devils are moving back in."

You want to fill up the empty spaces with God's Word. The Word of God is full of instruction on money. Memorize the scriptures to keep strong. You can begin with the scriptures found in this book.

One Final Word On What God Has Just Done In Your Life.

Do you remember when you got saved?

Do you remember how you may have said or done something that you shouldn't have? I know I did. **Immediately the devil tried to tell me that I wasn't saved.** He said if I had been "truly" saved, I would never have said or done what I did. Here's what I know to be true.

The spirit of debt has been broken out of your life and that's a fact.

"The devil is a liar, the father of lies and the truth is not in him."
        John 8:44

The devil is going to try to tell you that the spirit of debt and lack may be broken out of everybody else's life but not yours. Well, he's a liar. When you extend your faith, something supernatural takes place . . . the spirit of debt has been broken out of your life and that's a fact. LIVE in that freedom!

> When you extend your faith, something supernatural takes place . . . the spirit of debt has been broken out of your life and that's a fact.

QUESTIONS:

1. How do we know that all spirits must leave when commanded in the name of Jesus?

   _____

   _____

2. God has given us power in the spirit world; however, before any problem that arises from demon spirits can be solved, what must happen?

   _____

   _____

   _____

3. According to Luke 10:19, when we look up the meanings of *power*, we find we have _____ over all the _____ of the devil which means nothing can by any means hurt us!

4. What must be broken before you or anyone else can receive the full prosperity of God?

   _____

   _____

   _____

5. Is breaking the power of the spirit of debt nearly as hard as the devil would have you believe?

   _____

   What is the word of caution offered to keep you from re-accumulating debt?

   _____

   _____

Appendix

9 Questions To Ask
Before Going Into Debt

1.   Do I need it? Am I at peace in my spirit about this purchase?

Proverbs 1:5
"A wise man will hear, and will increase learning; and a man of understanding shall attain unto wise counsels."

Proverbs 1:7
"The fear of the Lord is the beginning of knowledge: but fools despise wisdom and instruction."

Proverbs 20:27 in the New Living Translation
"The Lord's searchlight penetrates the human spirit, exposing every hidden motive."

Proverbs 22:4 in the New Living Translation
"True humility and fear of the Lord lead to riches, honor, and long life."

Colossians 3:15
"And let the peace of God rule in your hearts, to the which also ye are called in one body; and be ye thankful."

2.   Is my spouse in agreement? How will it affect my wife? Husband? Children?

Proverbs 11:5 in the New Living Translation
"The godly are directed by their honesty; the wicked fall beneath their load of sin."

Proverbs 12:15 in the New Living Translation
"Fools think they need no advice, but the wise listen to others."

Amos 3:3 in the New Living Translation
"Can two people walk together without agreeing on the direction?"

Matthew 18:19
"Again I say unto you, That if two of you shall agree on earth as touching anything that they shall ask, it shall be done for them of my Father which is in heaven."

3.   Have I compared prices?   Will its value rapidly increase or decrease?   Does that matter?   Can I get along without the bells and whistles?   Would a less expensive item do as well?

Proverbs 13:16 in the New Living Translation
"Wise people think before they act; fools don't and even brag about it!"

Proverbs 20:14 in the New Living Translation
"The buyer haggles over the price, saying, "It's worthless," then brags about getting a bargain!"

Proverbs 27:23 in the New Living Translation
"Know the state of your flocks, and put your heart into caring for your herds."

4.   **Will I want this item as much next week, next month, next year, as I do today?** Delay does not mean denial.

Proverbs 27:12 in the New Living Translation
"A prudent person foresees the danger ahead and takes precautions. The simpleton goes blindly on and suffers the consequences."

Proverbs 27:20
"Hell and destruction are never full; so the eyes of man are never satisfied."

Ecclesiastes 3:1
"To everything there is a season, and a time to every purpose under the heaven."

5.   Will this purchase improve the quality of my life or that of my family? How often will I use it? Am I buying this for appearances, or to meet a need?

Proverbs 11:2 in the New Living Translation
"Pride leads to disgrace, but with humility comes wisdom."

Proverbs 12:9 in the New Living Translation
"It is better to be a nobody with a servant, than to be self-important but have no food."

Proverbs 12:26 in the New Living Translation
"The godly give good advice to their friends; the wicked lead them astray."

Proverbs 13:7 in the New Living Translation
"Some who are poor pretend to be rich; others who are rich pretend to be poor."

Proverbs 13:10 in the New Living Translation
"Pride leads to arguments; those who take advice are wise."

Proverbs 16:18 in the New Living Translation
"Pride goes before destruction, and haughtiness before a fall."

Proverbs 23:7 in the New Living Translation
"As a man thinks in his heart, so is he. . ."

6.   Do I have a plan to repay this debt rapidly? Is the plan written out with timetables? Can I wait and pay all or part of it in cash?

Proverbs 12:11 in the New Living Translation
"Hard work means prosperity; only fools idle away their time."

Proverbs 12:27 in the New Living Translation
"Lazy people don't even cook the game they catch, but the diligent make use of everything they find."

Proverbs 13:12
"Hope deferred maketh the heart sick: but when the desire cometh, it is a tree of life."

Proverbs 21:5
"The thoughts of the diligent tend only to plenteousness; but of every one that is hasty only to want."

Proverbs 21:5 in the New Living Translation
"Good planning and hard work lead to prosperity, but hasty shortcuts lead to poverty."

Proverbs 22:7
"The rich ruleth over the poor, and the borrower is servant to the lender."

Hebrews 6:12 in the New Living Translation
"Then you will not become spiritually dull and indifferent. Instead, you will follow the example of those who are going to inherit God's promises because of their faith and patience."

7.   Is this affordable in my present financial situation?   Am I buying this because it is on sale? Remember, if you can't afford it; it's not a good deal.

Proverbs 16:2-3 in the New Living Translation
"People may be pure in their own eyes, but the Lord examines their motives. Commit your work to the Lord, and then your plans will succeed."

Proverbs 21:20 in the New Living Translation
"The wise have wealth and luxury, but fools spend whatever they get."

Proverbs 22:27 in the New Living Translation
"If you can't pay it, even your bed will be snatched from under you."

8.   Have I considered the cost of owning this after I've paid the price for getting it? For instance, what will be the cost of upkeep and maintenance?

Proverbs 31:16 in the New Living Translation
"She goes out to inspect a field and buys it; with her earnings she plants a vineyard."

Luke 14:28 in the New Living Translation
"But don't begin until you count the cost. For who would begin construction of a building without first getting estimates and then checking to see if there is enough money to pay the bills?"

9.   Will this purchase help me in achieving God's goals for my life? Is there another way this goal could be met?

Proverbs 13:19 in the New Living Translation
"It is pleasant to see dreams come true, but fools will not turn from evil to attain them."

Proverbs 19:21 in the New Living Translation
"You can make many plans, but the Lord's purpose will prevail."

Proverbs 20:18 in the New Living Translation
"Plans succeed through good counsel; don't go to war without the advice of others."

9 Questions Quick Reference

1.   Do I need it? Am I at peace in my spirit about this purchase?

2.   Is my spouse in agreement? How will it affect my wife? Husband? Children?

3.   Have I compared prices? Will its value rapidly increase or decrease? Does that matter? Can I get along without the bells and whistles? Would a less expensive item do as well?

4.   Will I want this item as much next week, next month, next year, as I do today? Delay does not mean denial.

5.   Will this purchase improve the quality of my life or that of my family? How often will I use it? Am I buying this for appearances, or to meet a need?

6.   Do I have a plan to repay this debt rapidly? Is the plan written out with timetables? Can I wait and pay all or part of it in cash?

7.   Is this affordable in my present financial situation? Am I buying this only because it is on sale? Remember, if you can't afford it; it's not a good deal.

8.   Have I considered the cost of owning this after I've paid the price for getting it? For instance, what will be the cost of upkeep and maintenance?

9.   Will this purchase help me in achieving God's goals for my life? Is there another way this goal could be met?

31 Day Guide To Financial Freedom

Here is the way to get established in your new life.

For the next 31 days, read, absorb and take action over the following ways to change the way you look at and deal with money forever.

Don't get ahead of yourself.

Take one day at a time and you will develop the habit of looking, thinking and becoming wiser with the money you are trading your life for.

Harold Herring

DAY 1 - If I Were DEBT FREE, I would...

As you plan your future, it is important for you to ask yourself a very important question. "What would I do if I did not have any debt?"

Think carefully, then make a list of all the things you would do today if you did not owe a cent to anyone.

What would you do? Who would you bless? Would you invest more in feeding the hungry, clothing the naked, winning the lost or discipling the found? Would you help your relatives become debt-free? Would you secure a college education for your children or grandchildren? Take your time and record it below.

This is what I would do for God and my family if I were debt-free:

_____

_____

_____

_____

_____

_____

During this month, it is important for you to keep referring to this list. Make it your dream...your vision...your future.

132

POWER SCRIPTURES

"Where there is no vision, the people perish…."
Proverbs 29:18 A

"As we have therefore opportunity, let us do good unto all men, especially unto them who are of the household of faith."
Galatians 6:10

RICH THOUGHT

"You got to have a dream. If you don't have a dream, how you gonna have a dream come true?"
- "Happy Talk" from the musical South Pacific)
      lyrics by Oscar Hammerstein II

FUN QUOTE

"Don't be afraid to go out on a limb; that's where the fruit grows."
- Unknown

Harold Herring

DAY 2 - What Am I Exchanging My Life For?

Growing up in LaGrange, North Carolina, in a town of about 2,000 people, my parents owned a successful small business. My Dad didn't graduate from high school but was respected in our community as an honest, decent and hard-working man.

I will always remember the conversation he had with an older country gentleman who also owned a small business there. One day, the gentleman stopped by our store and asked my father to examine his financial records. He said he was having a problem with his business.

Out of a crumpled brown paper bag, he pulled an old ledger. As he opened it, my Dad noticed the words: "Tuck In" written on the upper corner of each left-hand page. The words "Tuck Out" were written on the upper corner of each right-hand page.

As my father tells the story, the old gentleman said, "Brother Harold, I think my problem is that I have 'tuck out' more than I have 'tuck in'." Almost everyone who lives in financial bondage got there because they "tuck out" more than they "tuck in."

Your first step to financial freedom is to find out where you are. Write down all your assets, listing everything you own. Place a practical fair market value on each item. Once you have done that, put down on paper everything you owe. List all your liabilities. Include loans to family members and any other obligations, even those you have been trying to forget. When you're done, subtract your liabilities from your assets and you will have your net worth.

If you divide your net worth by the number of years you have been employed, <u>you will discover how much you have been</u>

134

trading your life for each year. Don't get discouraged, because to begin any great journey, you must first know where you are. What is your starting point?

POWER SCRIPTURE

"Suppose one of you wants to build a tower. Will he not first sit down and estimate the cost to see if he has enough money to complete it? For if he lays the foundation and is not able to finish it, everyone who sees it will ridicule him, saying, 'This fellow began to build and was not able to finish'."
Luke 14:28-30 NIV

RICH THOUGHT

"Whenever we're afraid, it's because we don't know enough. If we understood enough, we would never be afraid."
- Renowned author and motivational speaker Earl Nightingale

FUN QUOTE

"Every day I get up and look through the Forbes list of richest people in America. If I'm not there, I go to work."
- Robert Orben, humorist

Harold Herring

DAY 3 - Detail All Outstanding Indebtedness.

Think IRS audit. Okay, now relax. I am not saying that you are going to be audited, but with an audit mindset, you probably would organize your files.

I want you to get every department store credit card, every bankcard and every bank statement that you have received over the past 12 months. Find all the stubs for your paychecks for that period, and last year's income tax return.

List your creditors, account numbers, phone numbers, outstanding balances, minimum payments, and interest rates. If it's a credit card, note whether or not that particular creditor charges an annual fee. Caution: During this exercise, don't worry about the total figures, because the enemy will try to discourage you from completing it. Remember that he is a liar, and is, in fact, the father of lies. You are simply recording numbers on a piece of paper so you can begin to have an intelligent discussion with your Heavenly Father.

Today, you will take the first powerful step toward positioning the enemy for a major attack. The ENEMY, by the way, is your DEBT.

Creditor	Monthly Payment	Amount Overdue	Monthly Amount I can afford	Interest Rate	Annual Fee

POWER SCRIPTURE

"...we will reap a harvest of blessing if we don't get discouraged and give up."
Galatians 6:9 TLB

RICH THOUGHT

"I have never met a man who has given me as much trouble as myself."
- 19th Century Evangelist Dwight L. Moody

FUN QUOTE

"When down in the mouth, remember Jonah. He came out all right."
- Thomas Edison

DAY 4 - Analyze Your Current Credit Position.

Total the credit card, department store, auto loan, personal loan and installment payments that you made over the past six months. (Do not include your mortgage payment.) Divide the total by six and you will have the average amount you spend on installment payments each month. The following chart will help you know where you are in controlling your debt.

Monthly Take-Home Pay	Amount You Should Spend Per Month In Installment Payments			
$	Excellent	Good	Fair	Poor
900	90	115	135	180
1,000	100	125	150	200
1,250	125	155	190	250
1,500	150	190	225	300
2,000	200	250	300	400
2,500	250	315	375	500
3,000	300	375	450	600
3,500	350	440	525	700
4,000	400	500	600	800
5,000	500	625	750	1,000
6,000	600	750	900	1,200
7,000	700	875	1,050	1,400
8,000	800	1,000	1,200	1,600

If your rating is *"Excellent"* or *"Good"* you can breathe easier. If your money is still funny, it is likely that the problem is discretionary or impulsive spending (eating out, entertainment, etc.).

A *"Fair"* rating means your financial condition is okay as long as the weather is fair. If financial clouds appear on the horizon, you are in trouble. You would not be able to handle the washing machine breaking down or an unexpected illness.

If your rating is *"Poor,"* you probably have the "late-notice blues" or "bill collector headaches." Fear not. Your condition is persistent but not permanent. You can be on the way up and on the way out of your dilemma by making some changes.

POWER SCRIPTURE

"Remember…that knowing what is right to do and then not doing it is sin."
James 4:17, TLB

RICH THOUGHT

"What is the difference between an obstacle and an opportunity? Our attitude towards it Every opportunity has a difficulty, and every difficulty has an opportunity."
-Anonymous

FUN QUOTE

"I've never been poor, but I've been broke, In fact, I've been so broke that when I walk by the bank, the burglar alarm goes off."
- Unknown

DAY 5 - Give Yourself a Raise.

Do you realize that three out of four employees overpay their taxes? That's right. The vast majority of taxpayers allow the government to use their money for a year, interest-free.

Every employee is responsible for completing a W-4 form upon being hired and/or when changes occur in their tax situation. The amount that is currently being withheld from your paycheck is called the withholding allowance. Seventy-five percent of taxpayers have more money withheld than is necessary. Some people like to get that tax refund every year, and feel that somehow they are pulling one over on the government. NOT TRUE. It's your money they are giving back to you. You should increase the number of allowances you can claim.

Would you like to increase your paycheck from $50 to $200 per month? Consider doing the following:

1. Call the payroll office to verify the number of allowances you currently have listed on your W-4 form.

2. Request a new W-4, and use the worksheet on the back of it to determine the number of allowances you should claim so that you will not be overpaying the government.

3. In completing the form, make sure you itemize all of last year's tax deductions. Include any IRAs and other deductions of this type. This will help you arrive at the proper number of allowances you should claim.

4. Return the completed form to your payroll department and eagerly anticipate your next paycheck. It should include the increased amount that you will be taking home.

5. NOW, use the increased take-home pay to pay off bills or invest it in a savings program. Do NOT go out and spend it!

If you are paying taxes every year on April 15, you are having too little money withheld and you need to decrease the number of allowances you are claiming.

POWER SCRIPTURE

"Good people leave an inheritance to their grandchildren, but the sinner's wealth passes to the godly."
Proverbs 13:22 NLT

RICH THOUGHT

"A person is truly poor, not when he has nothing, but when he does nothing."
- Anonymous

FUN QUOTE

"I have done an extensive survey . . . spared no expense . . . polled every possible demographic profile, and I have only found two groups of people that do not like to pay taxes: men and women."
- Unknown

DAY 6 - Go On a Money Diet.

If it isn't necessary, don't buy it. Talk with your family and let it become a family decision whether or not what you want to buy is really needed. Think of different ways you can save money. Pretend you're on a low-calorie, low-fat weight-loss diet, because debt, like extra weight, is tough to get rid of without plan and purpose.

Some cost-cutting strategies would be to:

Eat at home, not at a restaurant.

Cancel premium cable channels.

Discontinue cable TV altogether.

Cancel the newspaper subscription (buy Sunday's edition for the coupons).

Quit smoking.

Take the frills off your telephone plan especially if you are not using them.

Take your lunch to work.

Carpool to work.

Drink water rather than soft drinks or coffee.

These are only a few. Perhaps you can think of a few more.

POWER SCRIPTURE

"The wise man saves for the future, but the foolish man spends whatever he gets."
Proverbs 21:20, TLB

RICH THOUGHT

"Make all you can, save all you can, give all you can."
- John Wesley, founder of the Methodist movement

FUN QUOTE

If money talks, what it says most is good-bye.
- Unknown

DAY 7 - Your Church Should Challenge Your Faith.

Growing up in eastern North Carolina, I attended a church where my dad was a deacon and my mom taught Sunday School. Later, after I married, my wife taught the Senior High girls, but I was bored. I needed to have my faith challenged . . . I needed to be provoked . . . to understand God's promises and His covenant with His children.

When I found a church that challenged my faith, I changed.

You need to attend a church where the fullness of God's Word is taught. Sit under a pastor who can encourage, exhort and edify you through his teaching of the Bible. Pray . . . ask God where He wants you to worship. Once you become established there, get involved so you can function and flourish within that local Body of Christ.

Finally, remember that even God took a day of rest after working all week.

POWER SCRIPTURE

"Remember the Sabbath day, to keep it holy. Six days you shall labor and do all your work . . . For in six days the LORD made the heavens and the earth, the sea, and all that is in them, and rested the seventh day. Therefore the LORD blessed the Sabbath day and hallowed it."
Exodus 20:8, 9-11, NKJV

RICH THOUGHT

"In everything you do, put God first, and he will direct you and crown your efforts with success."
Proverbs 3:6, TLB

FUN QUOTE

"The Lord loves a cheerful giver until the giver begins to brag about it."
- Unknown

DAY 8 - Begin Calling Your Creditors.

Don't allow fear to cloud your decision to become debt free. Contact every creditor and explain to them your current financial situation. Work out an agreement for the amount that you can pay each month, including the date on which such payment would be due. Never promise to pay what you know you cannot!

If your situation is beyond your ability to become current, or to remain that way, consider asking one or more of your creditors to accept a smaller monthly payment. You could also ask if they would stop the interest accrual until you have become current. (All they can say is no.) **No matter how they respond to you, let your Christian character shine through. That is of paramount importance.**

Continue placing calls until you have spoken with all your creditors. Some of them will agree to your request. To those who do, send a letter thanking them and confirming what you have agreed to. To those who will not, go along with your plan, indicate that while some people declare bankruptcy to avoid paying their debts, you are hopeful that it will not be necessary in your case. The mention of bankruptcy will sometimes cause even the most cantankerous creditor to become more agreeable.

POWER SCRIPTURE

"In everything you do, stay away from complaining and arguing, so that no one can speak a word of blame against you."
Philippians 2:14-15, TLB

RICH THOUGHT

"Even a mistake may turn out to be the one thing necessary to a worthwhile achievement."
- automobile maker Henry Ford

FUN QUOTE

"I really don't like money but it calms my nerves."
- Joe Louis, boxer

DAY 9 - Rescue Your Money from Your Bank.

The average family overpays its bank more than $100,000 over the course of a 40-year relationship, borrowing for mortgages, home improvements and auto purchases, and using checking and savings accounts. This fact should put us in a sober frame of mind with which we will assess our own banking practices (Boardroom Classics; trademark of Boardroom Reports, Inc., NY, NY).

Some banks will hold a deposit until it has cleared or, worse, for a specified number of days, regardless of whether or not it has cleared. Make sure your deposits are credited to your account immediately. Withholding credit for more then 24 hours is unreasonable for this high-tech generation. An out-of-state check may require more time, but beware of unnecessary or excessive time restrictions. The bank is using your money and withholding your access to it in these situations. Watch them!

Consider the following banking suggestions:

1.   Find out the policies at your banking institution. This information is described in a brochure that can be obtained upon your request from your bank. For instance, it is helpful to know that at your bank, if you deposit a check after 4 p.m., it will not be reflected in that day's transactions. With this knowledge, you may avert incurring bounced-check fees. With the price of Non-Sufficient Fund (NSF) charges these days, this is information you need to know!

2.   Know whether fees will be assessed. If you write 25 checks and use the ATM 15 times in a month, with a service charge of $7.00 per month and .30 cents per ATM transaction, you are paying $19.00 per month or $228 per year. There is a better way to spend that money.

3. **Make your money work for you!** If your mortgage is through a particular bank, you will probably find they will give you much greater flexibility on your checking account. It is not untypical to be offered free checking or free checks, and a free saftety deposit box or all of these perks just for having your mortgage with them.

4. **Balance your bank statement every month.** Make sure all deposits were posted properly by the bank. BANKS DO MAKE MISTAKES. Also, it might be helpful, when you review your statement, if you would place a small star or "x" by every check that was written for a tax-deductible expenditure. You might even consider writing the "x" in red, so that it will stand out among your other register entries. When tax time rolls around, you will be glad you took a moment to do it.

Continued next on page . . .

Survey a number of banking institutions. Using the table below begin to chart the advantages and the disadvantages of each.

Bank Name				
Min. Balance for no service charge				
Amt. of Service Charge				
Per-Check Cost				
Stop Payment Fee				
Bounced Check Fee				
ATM Charge Your Bank				
ATM Charge Other Banks				

There is tremendous competition among banks today, so use that fact to your benefit.

To decide which one is best for you, review the statistics that you have found and decide where you want to bank.

Remember, it's your money!

POWER SCRIPTURE

"His Lord said unto him, Well done, thou good and faithful servant: thou hast been faithful over a few things, I will make thee ruler over many things: enter thou into the joy of thy Lord."
Matthew 25:21, KJV

RICH THOUGHT

"Do, or do not. There is no try."
- Yoda (of Star Wars fame)

FUN QUOTE

"If money doesn't grow on trees, then why do banks have branches?"
- Unknown

DAY 10 - The ATM Machine - "Absolutely Too Much."

Almost every grocery and convenience store and many gas stations now offer an ATM machine as a "customer service."

Each merchant charges a service fee, and your bank will sometimes charge an additional fee. The amount varies from $.50 to $5.00. There is big money in these fees which is why institutions have suddenly begun to impose this charge.

As far as I am concerned, *ATM* means:

<u>"Absolutely Too Much"</u>

You are charged absolutely too much to use it.

Find one of the many banks that does not assess a fee so long as you are using one of it's ATM machines.

POWER SCRIPTURE

"Dishonest money dwindles away, but he who gathers money little by little makes it grow."
Proverbs 13:11, TLB

RICH THOUGHT

"In life you are given two ends, one to think with and the other to sit on. Heads you win; tails you lose. You choose."
- Anonymous

FUN QUOTE

"You made a mistake, and I'm not going to pay for it."
- Criminal

"You going to use a credit card?"
- Sgt. Joe Friday Dragnet television show

DAY 11—Get a Better Credit Card.

How much of your hard-earned money do you "give away" in outstanding interest charges every month? Thirty-six percent of people paying credit-card interest are paying more than a 19% annual percentage rate (APR), when there are cards that are available with annual rates as low as 8.9%.

If you are paying high interest rates, call each card and ask them to be lowered. Ask the person who answers the phone if they are able to lower your interest rate. If they say no, ask to speak to a supervisor. Tell them you want to pay off the debt but you need help with a lower interest rate; most will oblige.

If you are not successful the first time, call again. There are thousands of persons and the likelihood of reaching the same person is astronomical and even if you do . . . ask again!

In selecting a low-interest credit card, all that glitters is not necessarily gold. There are a number of important questions you should consider in selecting a credit card. You will find some of the more important ones below.

Debt Determines Your Environment

	New Credit Card	Current Card	Current Card
Question 1: What is the interest rate? How long is that rate guaranteed?			
Question 2: Is there an annual fee? If so, How much?			
Question 3: Is there a grace period? If so, how many days?			
Question 4: Is there a fee for late payment? If so, how much?			
Question 5: Is there a fee for exceeding your credit limit? If so, how much?			
Question 6: Is there a fee for transferring other balances? How much?			

POWER SCRIPTURE
"A wise man thinks ahead; a fool doesn't, and even brags about it."
Proverbs 13:16, TLB

RICH THOUGHT
"A problem is a chance for you to do your best."
- composer/musician Duke Ellington

FUN QUOTE
A friend said he lost his credit cards six months ago. When asked if he had reported them stolen, he said, "No, the thief is spending less than we were, so we just let him keep them."
- Unknown

DAY 12 - Audit Your Life Insurance.

There are really only three basic types of life insurance policy, regardless of the fancy names given to them by insurance companies. There is *whole life*, which provides insurance, plus a way to accumulate cash value. There is *universal life*, which provides insurance and invests the cash value. And, there is *term insurance*, which is simply protection against loss of family income.

By definition, *insurance* is "coverage by contract whereby one party undertakes to indemnify or guarantee another against loss..." (Merriam-Webster.com). If you are in the market for insurance, you are looking for protection against lost income needed to provide for you or your family upon death. Term insurance provides the greatest amount of coverage for the least amount of dollars. The other two not only cost more, but they throw in another purpose for insurance

The question arises:
"What about cash value that I can borrow against at a very low-interest rate?"

The answer to that question is this one:
Whose money are you borrowing? If it's your cash, the insurance company is charging you interest to borrow your own money. If you need cash or cash growth, you need an investment.

Remember, insurance should be purchased only for insurance purposes, and only an investment should be handled as an investment.

It would be wise to examine all your policies, then for a quote contact:

SelectQuote at 800-963-8688 or www.SelectQuote.com

They will search their database, which includes more than 1,400 term-life insurance companies, and provide data so that you can make an informed decision. In any case, talk with an impartial party who could give you sound advice but would not be profiting from your decision.

POWER SCRIPTURE

"The rain came down, the streams rose, and the winds blew and beat against that house; yet it did not fall, because it had its foundation on the rock."
Matthew 7:25, NIV

RICH THOUGHT

"What you tolerate is what you live with."
- John Avanzini

FUN QUOTE

"Early to bed, early to rise, 'til you make enough money to do otherwise."
- Unknown

DAY 13 - It's Your Health and Your Money.

Thirty percent of health claims are denied each year because of minor errors. Half of those claimants simply accept the denial and never pursue payment again. A simple step in dealing with claims is to never accept "no" the first time you hear it. If you have a legitimate claim, take the time and energy to push for its payment or for a compromise.

If you have a medical policy, there are a number of ways to save money and save it now. A very realistic cost includes reducing the high price of prescription drugs. Even though the larger discount retail stores and discount drug stores offer lower prices, ask your doctor to recommend generic drugs. Build a relationship with a pharmacist and ask questions about those types of alternatives. Their schooling is in medicine, so their answers are often better than your physician's.

If your group or individual insurance policy offers different deductibles, take the higher one; it could reduce the amount you are paying monthly by as much as 30 to 45 %. With the savings, open a savings account and earmark it for future medical needs. It would be drawing interest along the way and you could also use it later for your deductible.

The Insurance Information Institute also handles insurance questions and provides excellent reports. Contact them at:

800-942-4242 (or 214-356-5500) or www.iii.org

This is a national service and they could help you with varying types of consumer information.

POWER SCRIPTURE

"Beloved, I pray that you may prosper in all things and be in health, just as your soul prospers."
3 John 2, NKJV

RICH THOUGHT

"Do what you can, with what you have, where you are."
- 26th U.S. President Theodore Roosevelt

FUN QUOTE

"I have enough money to last me the rest of my life, unless I buy something."
- comedian Jackie Mason

DAY 14 - Develop Your Own Confession of Faith.

Read, confess, meditate on and memorize scriptures that speak to your particular situation or need. Begin each day, not just Sundays, by confessing the Word over yourself, your family, your finances and your health.

When I wake up each morning, no matter where I am, the first thing I do is to say:

"Father, I thank you that you woke me up this morning. You clothed me in my right mind. You gave me air to breathe, a warm place to sleep, and food to eat. I thank you that I have a godly wife (who is so fine), four godly children, a godly daughter-in-love and two grandsugars. I thank You that the fruit of my body is blessed…that the blessings of the Lord will overtake me. I thank You that my blood pressure is 120 over 80 and that I walk in divine health…that I am above and not beneath…that I am the head and not the tail…that greater is He that is in me than he that is in the world. I thank You that I am debt-free…that there is going to be a miracle in my life TODAY, and anyone who comes near me is going to have a miracle in their life as well. Amen."

Develop your own confession from the Word of God.

Speak the pure, the powerful and the positive into your life.

Get it down in your spirit now!

POWER SCRIPTURE

"If any of you lack wisdom, let him ask of God, that giveth to all men liberally, and upbraideth not; and it shall be given him."
James 1:5

RICH THOUGHT

"No one would remember the Good Samaritan if he only had good intentions – he had money as well."
- Margaret Thatcher, 20th century British Prime Minister

FUN QUOTE

"Always remember it's better to give than to receive. That way you don't have to write thank-you notes."
- Unknown

DAY 15 - Use it or Lose it.

Everyone has "stuff" lying around that nobody will use again. Check all your clutter-accumulating spaces and locate everything that is not necessary or income producing.

One man's trash is another man's treasure, so if you are not using it, get rid of it. It could be just the item someone else has been looking for.

Have a garage sale, put it in the newspaper or on ebay to get the clutter out and the cash-flow in. Talk with some of your neighbors about having a neighborhood sale. The money you gain from it could be just the right "boost" you need to get rid of one nuisance bill.

Don't sell something you really want or something you would eventually end up replacing.

Remember, if it's not making you money, it is costing you money.

POWER SCRIPTURES

"…This place is too small for us; give us more space to live in."
Isaiah 49:20, NIV

"For who hath despised the day of small things?   for they shall rejoice…."
Zechariah 4:10, TLB

RICH THOUGHT

"Everything comes to him who hustles while he waits."
- inventor Thomas Edison

FUN QUOTE
"Be like the Mona Lisa.   She keeps smiling when her back's to the wall."
- Anonymous

Harold Herring

DAY 16 - Earn Extra Income.

Is there an extra job that you can secure for the short term?

To earn extra money, could you utilize one of your hobbies?

Consider selling cakes, sewing for others, landscaping, or something else you enjoy.

Don't despise small beginnings.

It could become an income producer.

Find something you enjoy doing and start doing it to earn extra income.

The only limitation you might face is your decision to take the first step.

POWER SCRIPTURE

"...let not your hands be weak and slack, for your good work shall be rewarded."
2 Chronicles 15:7 AMP

RICH THOUGHT

"Things turn out best for the people who make the best of the way things turn out."
- former basketball coach John Wooden

FUN QUOTE

"Robinson Crusoe started the 40-hour week. He had all the work done by Friday."
- Unknown

DAY 17 - Protecting Your Borders.

A popular phrase (especially before apartment and condo living) was, "*A man's home is his castle.*"

Throughout history men and women would take all kinds of measures to protect their homes and the possessions they had accumulated.

Times have changed since the days of digging moats around the outside walls to keep intruders out. But little has changed when it comes to the need to feel secure about protecting your possessions and your home – most often, your largest single investment.

Review your homeowner's policy, paying particular attention to the amount of your deductible. That amount is what YOU would pay before the insurance company would kick in to pay for your loss. (This amount could drastically vary from policy to policy.)

Remember, the HIGHER the deductible the LOWER the premium.

Keep in mind that the money you pay in premiums is YOUR MONEY.

POWER SCRIPTURE

"As for me and my house, we will serve the Lord."
Joshua 24:14

RICH THOUGHT
"Money-giving is a very good criterion of a person's mental health. Generous people are rarely mentally ill people."
- noted psychiatrist Dr.Karl A. Menniger

FUN QUOTE

"The reason I like money is that it goes with anything I wear."
- Anonymous

DAY 18 - Home, But Not "A Loan."

A homeowner can increase his net worth so easily that it may seem too good to be true. It isn't.

Calculate how much you should be spending on your home mortgage. For less than a dollar a day, you could save literally thousands of dollars on interest and cut years off your mortgage payments. Let me explain.

Let's say that Sam and Sally own a $100,000 home for which they are paying $665.30 each month (plus taxes and insurance) on their 30-year mortgage, at 7% interest.

If they were to add only $25 more per month as a principal payment, they would save $25,946 in interest and shorten their mortgage loan payments by three years and 10 months!

If Sam and Sally were to increase the amount to $200 a month in principal, they would save $72,695 in interest, which is thirteen years, eleven months in mortgage payments! It's like adding more than $72,695 to their net worth by paying off their own mortgage.

Not a bad investment return for $200 a month, and a great way to begin saving for retirement.

POWER SCRIPTURE

"I am the LORD your God, who teaches you to profit, who leads you in the way you should go."
Isaiah 48:17, NKJV

RICH THOUGHT

"Ninety-nine percent of failures come from people who have a habit of making excuses."
- agriculturist/inventor George Washington Carver

FUN QUOTE

"Getting ideas is like shaving: if you don't do it every day, you're a bum."
-Alex Kroll, two-time hall of famer

DAY 19—How Much House Can You Afford?

Are you ready for your dream home? *"With a small down payment and low, low monthly payments, you can move into your dream home quick and easy."* Does this ad sound familiar?

In the current economy, builders are making deals sound so good that it is difficult for many people to pass up the idea of owning their dream home. Unfortunately, the payments and the deal sound so easy that many unsuspecting consumers end up with a payment far greater than they can afford.

How much should you spend on your housing? Your limit for principal, interest, taxes, insurance and utility costs (electric, gas, water) should not exceed 28 percent of your annual gross income. Sure, you may feel that you can afford a higher payment, but what would happen in the event of unforeseen circumstances (job layoff or transfer, pregnancy, sickness)?

Buying a new home is very exciting, but don't let the excitement of the moment place you in bondage for the rest of your life.   In other words, don't let an enthusiastic salesperson or real estate agent tell you how much house you can afford.

Use the table on the next page to work it out. From the left column, choose the figure that best represents your gross annual household income. The maximum amount for housing appears in the column at the right.

Debt Determines Your Environment

Maximum Housing Allowance Based On Your Income

Annual Income	Maximum Housing Allowance
$ 15,000	$ 350
$ 20,000	$ 467
$ 25,000	$ 583
$ 30,000	$ 700
$ 40,000	$ 933
$ 50,000	$ 1,167
$ 60,000	$ 1,400
$ 75,000	$ 1,750
$ 100,000	$ 2,333

POWER SCRIPTURE

"Noah believed him even though there was then no sign of a flood, and wasting no time, he built the ark and saved his family…."
Hebrews 11:7, TLB

RICH THOUGHT

"Plans get you into things, but you gotta work your way out."
- humorist and actor Will Rogers

FUN QUOTE

"Money in the bank is like toothpaste in the tube. Easy to take out, hard to put back."
- baseball player Earl Wilson

DAY 20 - Who is Keeping Score on You?

Make sure your credit records are correct.

You should be aware that <u>24 out of 25 credit bureau files on individuals and businesses have errors</u> that can be quite costly. These errors can include everything from a simple twist of the facts by a tired employee or one dashing out to leave the office on time, to a major problem caused by careless "file mixing" (your files get mixed up with someone else's). Perhaps another person's name was the same as, or similar to, your own. **When someone's bad records get "blended" with your file, over time, you too begin to look bad.**

Because of the volume of data given to credit bureaus, there are bound to be some errors. **Most of the credit bureaus will send you a free copy of your report once a year**, so <u>take advantage of that and review your credit file annually</u> to ensure its accuracy.

<u>Beware companies who say they will provide a free report but want your credit card number first</u>. **Do not give it to them.**

POWER SCRIPTURE

"…those who seek the LORD shall not lack any good thing."
Psalm 34:10, NKJV

RICH THOUGHT

"I know God will not give me anything I can't handle. I just wish that He didn't trust me so much."
- missionary and humanitarian Mother Teresa

FUN QUOTE

"I don't want the cheese, I just want out of the trap."
- Spanish Proverb

DAY 21 - Financial Opportunities are Unlimited

Most people don't realize how much wealth there is in the world. People wonder why they can't get hold of a one-dollar bill, not realizing they are in short supply. There are more than 60 times as many one hundred dollar bills available as there are one-dollar bills. The amount of available wealth is staggering. Should we, as God's children, think that He would prefer to lavish it upon the sinner?

There are eight common minerals found under God's earth alone. If they were to be projected in value as they are mined over the next 20 years (with no adjustment for inflation), those eight would add Fifty-One Trillion, Four Hundred Eighty Billion Dollars of new wealth to the world economy. Worldwide coal reserves alone are figured at about Three Hundred Eighty-Three Trillion Dollars of wealth sitting beneath the earth's surface. This is but one small modicum of the available wealth, and yet the enemy gives chase to countless Christians who are trying to believe for a few hundred dollars a month.

The Word of God says that the Lord owns the cattle on a thousand hills (Psalm 50:10). The shortage is not God's; it's ours. Man's folly, caused by his ignorance of God's Word, causes shortages. A purchasing agent for a rich oil sheik once told me that when the sheik wants a McDonald's hamburger, he puts his entire family and crew into his 747 and off they fly to the nearest country that has a McDonald's restaurant. It might cost him $20,000 for one meal at McDonald's.

When the same sheik sends his wives to London to shop, he puts them in his private jet (an airborne palace, if you please) and burns up $17,500 worth of fuel. His wives have been known to spend a million dollars in the morning and two million in the afternoon on jewels, furs, shoes, furniture, cars, and other things. That is the wealth of only one man! We are limited in our perception of the vast wealth that God has provided in the earth. Concerning wealth and prosperity, the enemy loves to use deception on God's children. He knows we are the ones who will fund God's covenant. It is time for the saints of God to grasp this truth! The Word of God says, "*...this is the confidence with which we approach him, that whenever we ask anything that is in accordance with His will...we realize that we have what we have asked from him*" (1 John 5:14,15 TCNT). God wants His children to prosper.

These scriptures must take root in your spirit. Write them on 3 x 5 cards and take them wherever you go today and every day.

POWER SCRIPTURE

"...be not slothful, but followers of those who through faith and patience inherit the promises."
Hebrews 6:12, TLB

RICH THOUGHT

"Don't wait to be motivated. Take the bull by the horns until you have him screaming for mercy."
- educator and politician Michael Cadena

FUN QUOTE

"A lot of people are willing to give God the credit, but not too many are willing to give him the cash."
-Anonymous

DAY 22 - Avoid Financial Fender Benders.

If you audit your automobile insurance policy, you may find there are ways you can begin to save money, beginning today!

1. **Consider raising your deductibles.** Raising your comprehensive and collision deductible from $200 to $500 can reduce your premium up to 30 percent. If your current insurance bill is $1,000, you could realize close to a $350-a-year savings. Then take the savings and put the amount of your new deductible into a savings account. That way, if you do have an accident, you are prepared. If you don't have one, you have extra money in your retirement fund.

2. **Consider reducing your collision and comprehensive coverage if your car or truck is more than seven years old.** Some insurers are not obligated to repair your vehicle, but only to pay what it is worth at the time of the accident. This could leave you walking if your car is worth less than $1,000. If your auto insurance agent says you must have certain coverage in order to be licensed in your state, double-check with your local Department of Motor Vehicles to find out how much coverage is required.

3. **Explore what is available for you through your own health care plan and do not allow duplications in your auto insurance coverage.** Passenger health care is provided under the liability portion of your auto policy.

4. **Provision for a rental (and other extras) while your car is being repaired is a point-of-choice option.** If you are a two-car family, a rental would not always be necessary.

If you are getting close to paying off your auto loan, it is amazing how that same $300 payment (or more) would probably be absorbed in everyday expenditures almost without notice. There is a better way. <u>When the car is paid off, take the amount of the payment and begin putting it in a savings account toward the purchase of your next vehicle.</u>

POWER SCRIPTURE
"They imported a chariot from Egypt for six hundred shekels of silver."
2 Chronicles 1:17, TLB

RICH THOUGHT

"You said, 'but' I've put my finger on the whole trouble. You're a 'but' man. Don't say, 'but.' That little word 'but' is the difference between success and failure. Henry Ford once said, 'I'm going to invent the automobile,' and Arthur T. Flanken said, 'but....'"
- Sgt. Ernie Bilko, the Phil Silvers Show

FUN QUOTE

"Banks have drive-through windows so that the real people who own your car get to look at it three or four times a month."
- Unknown

DAY 23 - Audit Warranties and Service Contracts.

With every major purchase you make, a salesperson will try to persuade you to buy an extended warranty. They are available for virtually anything that sells for more than $100, and for a few items that sell for less than that. There are several reasons why the extended warranty on a vehicle is not the best investment you can make. The main reason is because extended coverage will not go into effect until the manufacturer's own warranty has run out.

Stop paying double. If your television comes with a one-year manufacturer's warranty, the seller gets the use of YOUR money for a full year, RISK FREE!

And then there is the extended protection policy on a freezer that comes from the manufacturer with a THREE-YEAR MANUFACTURER'S WARRANTY.

Why would anyone pay for an additional warranty for three years, when during that time period, the manufacturer has guaranteed to repair or replace the item(s) you purchased?

Here is the real kicker: When you add the cost of the extended policy to the total amount being financed, you are paying interest on a policy that in some cases won't go into effect for three years! Not only is this NOT a good use of your money, but it is thoughtless spending.

If you believe that you have such a policy, take it out and read it carefully.

POWER SCRIPTURE

"Give instruction to a wise man, and he will be yet wiser: teach a just man, and he will increase in learning."
Proverbs 9:9

RICH THOUGHT

"I do the very best I know how—the very best I can; and I mean to keep on doing so until the end."
- 16th U.S. President Abraham Lincoln

FUN QUOTE

"If you want to get back on your feet, just miss two car payments."
- Anonymous

DAY 24 - Can You Afford Your Car?

According to the National Automobile Dealers Association (NADA), it costs a family with a median annual income of $36,473 more than 26 weeks of earnings to buy a new car.

Upon leaving the dealer's showroom the value of the car immediately goes down dramatically. In developing your get-out-of-debt plan, consider buying a solid used car or dealer demo.

When buying a car, examine the loan value listed in the various car books, such as the Kelley Blue Book, the NADA Official Used Car Guide, and others.

Make every effort to never pay more than the value of the loan.

POWER SCRIPTURE

"I will instruct you (says the Lord) and guide you along the best pathway for your life; I will advise you and watch your progress."
Psalm 32:8, TLB

RICH THOUGHT

"The greatest thing in this world is not so much where we are but in what direction we are moving."
- poet Oliver Wendell Holmes

FUN QUOTE

"If you would like to buy an $40,000 car, it's easy—buy a $24,000 car on monthly payments."
- Unknown

DAY 25 - Know What's Under Your Hood.

Today is the day to begin to increase your knowledge about how to take care of your car. Below are some very basic maintenance checks that can preserve the life of your vehicle and its parts.

1. **Four out of five vehicles operate just as efficiently on 87 octane gasoline**, with no significant effect on fuel economy, durability or emissions, according to the U.S. Department of Energy. There is usually a four to six cents difference between 87 and 89 octane, and an eight to twenty cents difference between 87 and 92 octane gasoline. If you burn 20 gallons of fuel per week, you could realize a savings of $40 to $208 per year.

2. **When you are traveling by car, always refuel where the truckers stop and shop.** These professional drivers always know the best places. Avoid buying gas at the time a station is receiving a delivery of fuel. As the gasoline pours into the holding tank, it stirs up the sediment. This is bad news for your engine. Also buy early in the morning when the weather is cooler. Heat expands fuel and you get less than what you paid for.

3. **Run your car's air conditioner at least 10 minutes every week.** Frequent use of the air conditioner, regardless of the outside temperature, will maintain coolant pressure and greatly reduce the possibility of costly repairs.

4.   **Avoid using the "255" air conditioning system** *(two windows down at 55 miles per hour)*. The wind-resistance experienced by your car could reduce your gasoline performance by up to five miles per gallon.

Do yourself a favor, organize the maintenance information on your car. It may be a clunker, but it's your clunker for now. If you want God to bless you with another car, prove that you are faithful in caring for the one you have.

POWER SCRIPTURE

"If ye know these things, happy are ye if ye do them."
John 13:17

RICH THOUGHT

"You may try to destroy wealth and find that all you have done is increase poverty."
- British Prime Minister Winston Churchill

FUN QUOTE

"If you think you will not be missed, move away leaving a few unpaid bills."
- Unknown

DAY 26 - Begin a Systematic Savings Plan.

After you pay your tithes, you should pay yourself. Put 10% of your income into a savings plan.

This may seem like an impossible task, but it is imperative that you start somewhere.

Take heart. The simple act of making a decision to do something is your first step in the right direction.

Recognize your need and make a commitment toward it.

Make saving become your lifestyle. If you will do that, you will enjoy watching the amount increase over time.

POWER SCRIPTURE

"Consider [the ant's] ways and be wise! It...stores its provisions in summer and gathers its food at harvest."
Proverbs 6:6-8

RICH THOUGHT

"...you can change where you are by changing what goes into your mind."
- Zig Ziglar

FUN QUOTE

"The Eiffel Tower is the Empire State Building after taxes."
- Unknown

DAY 27 - It's a Matter of WILL Power

Do you have a will? Where is it? Do your heirs and/or beneficiary(ies) know where it is?

Part of planning ahead is writing your will because there are numerous things to consider. You may not think you have much, but make provision in a will to ensure that if something happens to you, what you leave behind will end up where you want it.

If you have children that are still dependent upon you, there is another very important part of planning involved. You must seriously consider who will take care of them in the event that both parents are deceased.

While we may feel the pressures of regaining our independence over debt, we have a larger concern than even amassing the money itself. If we have provision for our children, have we chosen someone who will minister to our children emotionally as well as financially?

The thought of leaving dependent children behind is such a difficult one that most couples and single parents never come to a final decision. This matter is often left unanswered or unaddressed. The best-qualified people to make this important decision, though, are the parents not the courts.

Answering the questions above may involve some important prayer time. Decisions concerning minors must be spirit-led because we are spirit beings (John 3:3). We are capable of making the right decisions if we permit God to lead.

186

POWER SCRIPTURE

"Lazy hands make a man poor; but diligent hands bring wealth."
Proverbs 10:4, NIV

RICH THOUGHT

"When you discover your mission, you will feel its demand. It will fill you with enthusiasm and a burning desire to get to work on it."
- self-made billionaire/philanthropist W. Clement Stone

FUN QUOTE

"Crows fly in flocks while eagles fly alone."
- German writer/scientist   Johann Goethe

MAY 28 - Does God Want Me to Plan Ahead?

Proverbs 13:22 says, "*A good man leaves an inheritance to his children's children*" (NKJV). Good people are those who have lined up their lives with the Word of God. If we are expected to leave an inheritance for our grandchildren, that is no small thing.

God's Word also says, "*Steady plodding brings prosperity, hasty speculation brings poverty*" (Proverbs 21:5).

People misunderstand the concept of being wealthy. It would surprise many to realize that, statistically, most millionaires don't buy their homes in exclusive neighborhoods where they can afford to live and they don't own the luxury vehicles that they can afford to drive. For example, the late Sam Walton, founder of the successful Wal-Mart store chain, drove around in a pick-up truck. Wealthy people like Mr. Walton are comfortable and realize that wealth does not necessarily mean having the best of everything. Wealth is what you keep, not what you spend. It is a collection of assets, not things. It's more "attitude" than "acquisition."

The Word of God explains this principle in James 4:3: "*And even when you do ask, you don't get it because your whole motive is wrong—you want only what will give you pleasure.*"

Those who seek riches for themselves will never find them because they cannot resist the temptation to spend. The "steady plodding" referred to in the book of Proverbs, brings true wealth to the believer, so that he not only might "*establish God's Covenant in the earth*" (Deuteronomy 8:18), but that he might also leave an inheritance for his grandchildren.

Retirement will not take care of itself. You must decide where you want to go, and then plan how to get there. Most of us are so caught up in the intenseness of our "today" that we don't take the time to plan ahead. According to statistics, most Americans have only an average of $2,000 saved by age 65. At that age, it's a bit late to think about saving for retirement.

Give some thought today as to what you would like to put aside for building your future. Write down what you have that is already working on your behalf. It might be good as well, to write down what is not working and attempt to correct that.

POWER SCRIPTURE

"For I know the plans I have for you...to give you a future and a hope."
- Jeremiah 29:11, NIV

RICH THOUGHT

"There would be no advantage to be gained by sowing a field of wheat if the harvest did not return more than was sown."
- motivational speaker/businessman Napoleon Hill

FUN QUOTE

"Saving is a very fine thing, especially when your parents have done it for you."
- British Prime Minister Winston Churchill

DAY 29 - Pay Off Debts Quickly.

If you have a credit card with a $1,000 balance at 21% interest, it would take you 138 months (more than 11 years) to eliminate it if you make only the minimum required payment (not to mention that you would pay $1,104.63 in interest on a $1,000 loan!).

If you pay an extra five dollars a month, you can cut the time from 138 months to 58 months, and save $438.66 in interest. Paying an additional $10 a month would save you 81 months and $621.95 in interest.

Most Americans are lulled to sleep by the devil as he steals the very lifeblood of their savings. This could be a very powerful strategy in your war on debt.

POWER SCRIPTURE

"Look straight ahead; don't even turn your head to look. Watch your step. Stick to the path and be safe."
Proverbs 4:25-26, TLB

RICH THOUGHT

"When life knocks you down, try to land on your back, because if you can look up, you can get up."
- motivational speaker and author Les Brown

FUN QUOTE

"The exercise that wears most people out is running out of cash."
- Anonymous

DAY 30 - Plan a "Cash Day."

Wow! What an exciting concept! A cash day! Go, cash!

Yes, that's right. You have planned for it, and if you think really hard, there probably has been a day in the past when you have actually done it. You have actually gone through an entire day without using a credit card, debit card, or writing a check. Why not try to end every day without using any of these forms of payment?

"But I make all my purchases by check," you say. "Isn't that like cash?" Yes and No. Have you ever played the float? That is, have you ever written a check when the money wasn't in the bank, but you knew that your deposit would beat the check to the bank? Those are the first bricks in constructing a foundation of false security.

Writing a check to a vendor when there is no money in the bank is not a game; it's against the law. You are taking a risk, so stop kidding yourself! Don't insult God by writing a "faith check," when in reality it's a "fake check." I understand the intent. There was a time in my life when I not only robbed Peter to pay Paul, but I also asked James, Andrew and John for a loan, so I know what it's like to be broke. But, it's fraudulent to write a check when sufficient funds are not in your account to cover it.

Pay cash . . . it will teach you some powerful lessons about money.

POWER SCRIPTURE

"As [a man] thinketh in his heart, so is he."
Proverbs 23:7

RICH THOUGHT

"There were many times my pants were so thin I could sit on a dime and tell if it was heads or tails."
- actor Spencer Tracy

FUN QUOTE

"Don't worry about keeping up with the Joneses; they just declared Chapter 13 bankruptcy."
- anonymous

DAY 31 - It's Working!

By now, you should see a recognizable difference in the way you handle money matters - or in the way you plan to handle them. Review your progress and the money you've saved. Note your accomplishments as they happen.

"Then those who feared the Lord talked together, and the Lord paid heed and listened. A record was written before him of those who feared him and kept his name in mind." (Malachi 3:16 (NEB)

There are times when we must strengthen ourselves in the Lord as the Psalmist David did (1 Samuel 30:1-6). We need to write down our victories in a journal or notebook so at any time we will be able to say, "Look what the Lord has done!" Every time a bill is paid off or even at certain intervals along the way, choose a page over which the family can celebrate. They will gain encouragement, as will you, from the progress you are making. It is great to have praise and worship time before the Lord when He has delivered you from something or when you have experienced victory in some area.

For the past 30 days, you have concentrated on your commitment to become debt-free. You have spent time thinking about it, gathering information to plan it, and deciding how exciting the alternative or result is going to be. Statistics show that if we do anything for at least 20 consecutive days, it will become a habit. In this way, we can actually create a new habit to replace a former one.

THE BATTLE PLAN IS UNFOLDING!

POWER SCRIPTURE

"Quit praying and get the people moving! Forward march!"
God speaking to Joshua in Exodus 14:15, TLB

RICH THOUGHT

"Money is not bad. There is not anybody I know who really thinks it's bad. If they do, why don't they give back their paycheck?"
- Dr. Charles Stanley; First Baptist, Atlanta, GA

FUN QUOTE

"Even if you're on the right track, you'll get run over if you just sit there."
- humorist and actor Will Rogers

Debt Determines Your Environment

Invite Harold Herring to speak
at your church, event, or conference.

Email Harold at:

booking@haroldherring.com

or call 1-800-583-2963   ext 100

With a mix of humor, practical strategies, and Biblical insight Harold will inspire, encourage, and prepare you to change your financial destiny. Let him set you on the path to debt freedom and the life God is calling you to. Remember, you are never truly free until you are financially free.

RichThoughts Weekly Email

Right Now Practical Strategies for Saving Money

Biblical Insights on Increasing Your Finances

RichThoughts Video and 2 Minute Video

Thought Provoking Humor

These are just a few of the things you are missing if you're not signed up for the **RichThoughts Weekly Email**.

To sign up visit:
www.RichThoughts.org
and get ready to be inspired, encouraged, and entertained.

Debt Determines Your Environment

THE
GUARANTEED
CDs

Scriptural strategies and proven financial principles which are responsible for saving thousands of people millions of dollars in interest and debt.

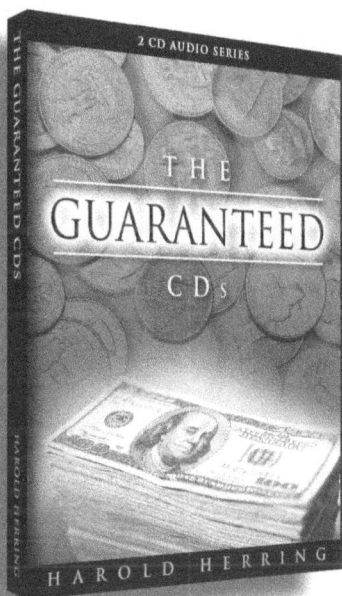

- 2 hours of teaching
- Powerful insights
- Easy-to-implement strategies
- Real answers to the money problems you're facing

"Gonna recommend . . . to everyone I know . . . I did save $500 just like you said!!"
- Sherrice, Louisville, KY

$19.95 + S&H

www.debtfreearmy.org/store
or call 1-800-583-2963 ext. 100

MONEY BACK GUARANTEE

I, Harold Herring, personally GUARANTEE that implementing the strategies taught on these two CDs will save you a minimum of $500 within the first thirty days of purchase. If not, your money will be promptly refunded upon receipt of your written request and the return of this album and the CDs.